P9-DHE-052

RUDOLF BULTMANN

Makers of the Modern Theological Mind
Bob E. Patterson, Editor

Makers of the Modern Theological Mind
Bob E. Patterson, Editor

RUDOLF BULTMANN

by Morris Ashcraft

Word Books, Publisher, Waco, Texas

First Printing—August 1972
Second Printing—December 1975

RUDOLF BULTMANN

Copyright © 1972 by Word Incorporated, Waco, Texas 76703. All rights reserved. No part of this book may be reproduced in any form, except for brief quotations in reviews, without the written permission of the publisher.

Printed in the United States of America
Library of Congress catalog card number: 74-188059

Dedicated to the memory
of
my beloved mother
Ida Matthews Ashcraft

Editor's Preface

Who are the thinkers that have shaped Christian theology in our time? This series tries to answer that question by providing a reliable guide to the ideas of the men who have significantly charted the theological seas of our century. In the current revival of theology, these books will give a new generation the opportunity to be exposed to significant minds. They are not meant, however, to be a substitute for a careful study of the original works of these makers of the modern theological mind.

This series is not for the lazy. Each major theologian is examined carefully and critically—his life, his theological method, his most germinal ideas, his weaknesses as a thinker, his place in the theological spectrum, and his chief contribution to the climate of theology today. The books are written with the assumption that laymen will read them and enter into the theological dialogue that is so necessary to the church as a whole. At the same time they are carefully enough designed to give assurance to a Ph.D. student in theology preparing for his preliminary exams.

Each author in the series is a professional scholar and theologian in his own right. All are specialists on, and in some cases have studied with, the theologians about whom they write. Welcome to the series.

Bob E. Patterson, Editor
Baylor University

CONTENTS

7

I. Rudolf Bultmann

Rudolf Bultmann, professor of New Testament in the University of Marburg, retired in 1951, but his is still the most frequently discussed name in theological circles. His long shadow continues not only in New Testament studies, but extends into other theological disciplines. He stands alongside Karl Barth as a man who changed the direction of theology significantly and perhaps permanently. Both men were nurtured in the liberal tradition. Barth attracted the attention of the theological world when he wrote his commentary on Paul's letter to the Romans. This publication marked the turning point from liberalism to a new Reformation theology— neoorthodoxy or dialectical theology—and catapulted Barth's name into prominence between the World Wars. Bultmann stood with Barth in the new dialectical theology, but proceeded with his new method of interpretation to change theological understanding even more radically. Since World War II, Bultmann has been the center of the discussion in theology.

Bultmann's prominence is related primarily to this new kind of biblical interpretation. But his writings in other areas are also worthy of recognition. He is a recognized authority in the history of religions, the philosophy of religion, and in theology, as well as in New Testament and methods of interpretation. His new method of interpretation was largely inspired by his own commitment to Christian faith and by the

difficulty of interpreting it in the modern scientifically orient-
ed culture. Bultmann, a completely convinced modern scientific man, was sympathetic to those who found the strange
religious language of the New Testament quite unintelligible.
He developed his method of interpretation and applied it
thoroughly and consistently during an entire generation in an
effort to make Christian faith understandable to modern men.
Herein is his claim to fame.

At first glance, his method appears to be somewhat vague
and difficult. The terminology is strange. But beyond the difficulty there is the obvious and reassuring evangelistic fervor
of a Christian scholar who believes in Christ and seeks to
make his message known. He chose a method based on an
understanding of human existence which, in his judgment,
was in keeping with that found in the New Testament. It is
called existentialist interpretation.

Although a more thorough discussion of Bultmann's distinctive terms will be presented later, a brief definition of
"existentialist" is in order now. The term is derived from the
word "existence" as it is used in the general term "existentialism." One should not think of existentialism as a clearly
defined system of philosophy, because there is considerable
diversity among the existentialists. It is better to look upon
existentialism as a way of thinking which is based upon the
concept of existence. Sören Kierkegaard, the Danish philoso-
pher (1813–1855), was the father of what is now known as
existentialism. He was offended by Hegelian philosophy which
by exalting reason reduced all reality to reason. To Kierkegaard, the assertions of rationalism were not only inadequate
but also arrogant. He argued that reason was only one aspect
of reality. For instance, man is endowed with love, fear, anxiety, and hope, as well as with reason. Reason tends to be
objective and can easily become disinterestedly analytical.
But real human life is primarily subjective, because love,
fear, anxiety, hope, and joy are its components and they are
not primarily rational. In other words, one knows more about
reality in the nonrational, subjective, and individual involve-

ment in life than he does by general, objective reason. In fact, human existence is much more complex and meaningful than can be apprehended rationally. Kierkegaard rejected the supremacy of reason as an understanding of reality and chose the broader base of existence.

An illustration may help, even though it tends to distort by oversimplifying. Let us suppose that I am in my study working on this manuscript. A friend appears at my door and announces that a young girl has just been struck by an auto at a nearby intersection. I may be moved to sympathy for the girl and her family. I may think about what could be done to relieve the traffic congestion. I may even organize or join in some effort to reduce the number of such accidents. But soon with the unpleasant, but generally held, conviction that such accidents are inevitable I resignedly return to my writing. However, let us suppose that my friend had reported that the girl's name was Anna Belle. The addition of this one detail changes both the message and the situation which follows. Anna Belle is my daughter. The message is no longer general. It is quite specific. It involves me. This message is no occasion for reflection, objective analysis, or even sympathy. It threatens and involves my entire existence. It has such mass that it draws reason into its appropriate orbit in harmony with fear, anxiety, faith, hope, and the other characteristics of existence. I respond to this message. I do not analyze it. I respond in my entire existence. This is existential response.

Existentialist Bultmann thinks that the message of the New Testament is this kind of event. It is an event in a message addressed to me. If I respond with curiosity, or even interest, and reflect on its reliability, I have missed the entire point. Christ appeared to the men of his generation, and they sensed that they had been brought into God's presence. Everything changed. Their counterfeit lives were transformed into authentic existence. Their shackles were removed and they were free for the first time. This happened when they came to faith in Christ. Their response was existential.

As a devout Lutheran Christian, Bultmann believes that

this happens today when men really "hear" the Christian gospel. He set out to develop a method of interpretation which would open this door to modern man. In Kierkegaard's idea of existence he found what appeared to him to be the New Testament understanding of existence. In Martin Heidegger's philosophy, of which we shall hear more later, he found a comprehensive system of concepts and terms which afforded him the approach he needed. Bultmann used these concepts and terms in developing his own method of interpretation.

One illustration is the much-publicized "demythologizing." Bultmann regards the world view in the New Testament as mythological. Apparently, the writers thought that the universe consisted of a three-story structure: heaven, earth, and the underworld. God and the angels lived in heaven. Satan and the demons lived in the underworld. Man lived on the earth in-between and was likely to be visited, or invaded, for good or ill from above or below. When the writers described these invisible "other-worldly" powers in "this-worldly" language they were using the language of myth.

Furthermore, Bultmann maintains that a modern man with his scientific view of the universe could not believe in the mythological world view even if he wanted to. To insist that one must accept the New Testament world view in order to accept the Christian message would be both impossible and preposterous. Modern man knows more about the world and has a better explanation for illness than demons. Then, how can modern man understand that New Testament message? Bultmann replies that the New Testament message must be demythologized.

But to demythologize the New Testament does not mean that one strips away the myth. Rather, it means that the New Testament message must be interpreted existentially. This is so because the writers of the New Testament were intending to describe not the architecture of the universe but the facts of their own existence. They were expressing their convictions that they were not lords of their own existence, that the world had an origin and meaning beyond itself, and that Christ had delivered them from invisible powers. In short, their message was about their own existence, and only their language was mythological. To understand their existence and to interpret that meaning is existentialist interpretation, or demythologizing, which in this instance is the same.

Historians cannot agree yet as to how they will appraise Bultmann's efforts. But they do agree that he has faithfully and consistently applied his method, and that he has changed theological studies at least for a generation.

BIOGRAPHICAL SKETCH

Rudolf Bultmann is a churchman. It is not surprising that he has given his life to the church. He was a product of the church, born August 20, 1884, in Wiefelstede of Oldenburg, Germany, the oldest son of Arthur Bultmann who was at that time the Evangelical Lutheran pastor in the town. Arthur Bultmann had been born in Freetown, Sierra Leone, West Africa, while his parents were serving as missionaries. Rudolf's maternal grandfather had been a pastor in Baden.

Bultmann's entire life has been focused on the fields of theology and biblical studies. Seemingly, he never contemplated any other career and never interrupted his work for other endeavors. His elementary schooling was in Rastede (1892–95). He attended the *Gymnasium* in Oldenburg (1895–1903). In his "Autobiographical Reflections," he spoke of his school days as having been most pleasant.[1]

He began his study of theology in 1903 in the University of Tübingen. After three semesters, in keeping with the European practice of studying in several universities, he went to the University of Berlin for two semesters, and later to Marburg for two semesters. He took his first theological examination in Oldenburg in 1907 and then taught in the *Gymnasium* for one year. In 1910 he was awarded his degree (Lic. theol.) by the University of Marburg. His second research dissertation, which qualified him to be an instructor in the theological faculty, was completed in 1912. From that date until 1916 he lectured in New Testament at the University of Marburg.

Bultmann held professorships in three universities. From 1916 until 1920 he was assistant professor at the University of Breslau. During his time in Breslau he was married and his first two daughters were born. His youngest brother was killed in France in 1917, and Bultmann suffered the privations of a country defeated by war. In 1920 he moved to Giessen as a professor, but remained only one year before returning to his alma mater in 1921. He succeeded his old teacher Wilhelm Heitmüller in the New Testament chair in Marburg and remained in that position until his retirement in 1951. Since 1951, as professor emeritus, Bultmann has continued to be very active in writing and lecturing.

Bultmann's modesty is obvious in his autobiographical sketch and in the fact that there is a scarcity of biographical material about him. He has, in spite of world-wide fame, remained personally in the background while his thoughts have been presented, debated, and evaluated. In his autobiographical sketch, he did not even mention the essay on "demythologizing." This is also indicative of his own evaluation of its importance. Actually, that essay got the attention of the world but the method of interpretation is obvious in his earlier works.

Rather frequently, Bultmann acknowledged particular indebtedness to several of his teachers. Of particular importance were Johannes Weiss and Wilhelm Herrmann. Weiss, famous as a New Testament scholar in the History of Religions School, guided Bultmann in his graduate study and doctoral preparation. Herrmann was the acknowledged systematic theologian of the liberal theological movement in which Bultmann began his work. Bultmann departed from the liberal school, but he never ceased to express gratitude to his teacher Herrmann. Bultmann also acknowledged his gratitude to Adolf Harnack, the church historian, to Hermann Gunkel, the Old Testament scholar, both of the University of Berlin, and to Karl Müller of Tübingen and to Adolf Jülicher of Marburg.

Bultmann is held to be quite radical in his theological and hermeneutical methods by many of his English readers. Nevertheless, the more one learns of and from Bultmann, the more he is impressed by the stability and consistency which characterize his whole life and writings. For instance, Bultmann moved from liberal theology into the dialectical theology associated with the name of Karl Barth, but in such a way that he never turned against his teachers of the liberal school and never ceased to appreciate his liberal heritage. At the same time, he advocated many of the major themes of dialectical theology, but never did he make any radical switches or changes of direction. Furthermore, his consistency in thought spans more than half a century, and the ideas he expressed in the 1920s are reaffirmed and deepened in his writings of the 60s, but are strikingly unchanged.

Students frequently ask how Rudolf Bultmann remained in a German university during the Hitler regime when Karl Barth and Paul Tillich were forced to leave Germany, Martin Niemöller was imprisoned, and Dietrich Bonhoeffer was imprisoned and killed. It is with reluctance that I mention this question, lest I do harm to the life of a great man who lived in a difficult setting which can hardly be understood by an outsider. Perhaps the clue to understanding this question is to be found in Bultmann's "Autobiographical Reflections," in which he said, ". . . I have never directly and actively participated in political affairs." [2] Furthermore, Bultmann participated in the formation and continuation of the Confessing Church, which was organized by those churchmen who were unwilling for the church to become an agent of Nazism. [3] He signed the Barmen Declaration. On May 2, 1933, he departed from his stated precedent long enough to enunciate his attitude about some problems of the Hitler regime then before the German people. In a lecture to his students, he denounced the defamation of the German Jews, but did not specifically condemn Hitler.[4]

Walter Schmithals, a friend and student of Bultmann who has written a superb introduction to Bultmann's thought, cites other occasions on which Bultmann maintained his Christian stance in Hitler's Germany. On one occasion, the General Synod of the Lutheran Church passed a regulation concerning the appointment of pastors and other church officials which required not only the candidate's unconditional support of the state but also that the candidate and his wife be of Aryan descent. On September 19, 1933, the Marburg faculty unanimously opposed these provisions in a statement written for the most part by Bultmann. In his sermons of 1937 and 1938 Bultmann spoke specifically and disapprovingly of the current nationalistic myths and acts which stood in contrast to the Christian way.[5]

Bultmann's numerous and significant publications span half a century. No attempt will be made at this time to list them, but the more pivotal writings will be mentioned in connection with the following discussion of the theological climate in which Bultmann lived and the issues to which he responded.[6]

THE THEOLOGICAL CONTEXT OF BULTMANN'S CAREER

Bultmann was educated in, accepted, and cherished until at least 1920 the liberal theology which had developed in the nineteenth century. Liberal theology was characterized by an openness to truth and the employment of scientific methods in research. It tended to break away from tradition unless other grounds than tradition could be found for keeping previously held ideas. Liberals were skeptical of claims about ultimate truth, and regarded their own conclusions as tentative. They applied the principle of continuity in the study of the Christian faith, and therefore tended to interpret its content in the light of outside influences and causative factors. The liberals tended to emphasize the immanence of God in preference to his transcendence. They were optimistic about man and believed in his progress. To most of them, Jesus was the focus of Christian thought and the legitimate object of the "historical quest," which produced a kind of sentimental attachment to Jesus and a noticeable disinterest in Christological problems. Liberal theology stressed social justice and brought about some of the more desirable reforms of the twentieth century.

Adolf Harnack, though a church historian by specialty, wrote what became the popular summary of liberalism, a little book entitled *What Is Christianity?* Bultmann wrote the introduction to the new (1950) edition of this book because he thought every theological student should read it in order to understand the present theological situation. However, he criticized Harnack for missing both the importance of the History of Religions School and the eschatological consciousness of the New Testament. He thought Harnack "diluted to the point of harmlessness" the problematical core of Christian faith.[7] It was this kind of liberalism exemplified by Harnack's oversimplification that Bultmann abandoned when he went with Karl Barth into the new dialectical theology. However, he retained many of liberal theology's characteristics and contributions.

The History of Religions School was one development in the liberal tradition from which Bultmann learned much and to which he made a significant contribution in his later work (1949) *Primitive Christianity in its Contemporary Setting.*[8] In this book, Bultmann portrays Jesus as belonging to Judaistic rather than Christian thought, and interprets much of early Christianity in terms of Gnosticism.

One cannot understand Bultmann without understanding his use of form criticism. This method of research reflects the liberal appreciation for scientific method. Bultmann, along with K. L. Schmidt and Martin Dibelius, developed and applied this method to New Testament study as Gunkel had done in the study of the Old Testament. The form critics assume that the Gospel contents first circulated as small and independent units which, under community influence, developed according to discoverable laws of form. They assume that in the period of oral tradition, prior to the written Gospels as we have them, the chronological, geographical, and transitional statements were added by the editors. The most helpful clue toward understanding Gospel material is to discover the "life situation" of the early community which called forth, used, interpreted, and preserved the particular narrative. A scientific study of the material following the guidelines of form criticism would allegedly show what actually happened and was said.[9]

Bultmann's first major work was *The History of the Synoptic Tradition*, published in 1921,[10] one of the classics in the form criticism tradition. It received much opposition for many years, but has become something of a requirement in the critical study of the Gospels. Its importance can hardly be exaggerated. This book appeared to be so clearly in the liberal tradition that Karl Barth was amazed when Bultmann, so shortly thereafter, favorably reviewed his own sensational commentary on Romans which broke radically with the liberal tradition.

Dialectical theology is generally regarded as having begun with Karl Barth's *Römerbrief*.[11] Bultmann, as has been noted, looked favorably upon this publication and regarded himself in the same theological movement with Barth and Friedrich Gogarten. His own writings of the period show that he had come to differ with liberal theology in several essentials. In his 1924 essay, "Liberal Theology and the Latest Theological Movement," he indicated that liberal theology had made man the center of theology rather than God. To him, and other dialectical theologians, God is the subject of theology.[12] Liberal theology, with its primary emphasis on history, had searched for the historical Jesus and had sought to ground faith in historical objectivity. Bultmann rejected these conclusions and argued that historical research must never be understood as a basis for faith, since its conclusions have only relative validity.[13] Along with the quest for the historical Jesus, Bultmann refused the "liberal" Jesus, the pantheistic idea of God often found in liberal theology, and the optimistic view of man. He rejected what he called the "pantheism of history" found in liberal theology, because it pretended to know God directly. He maintained that God is not an entity and cannot, therefore, be known as objects are known.[14]

In his 1928 essay, "The Significance of 'Dialectical Theology' for the Scientific Study of the New Testament," he indicated that he shared certain convictions with dialectical theology, such as the radical difference between God and man, the necessity for revelation, and the importance of the Word. However, Bultmann always charted his own course and never followed some other guide. To him dialectical theology was not a set of doctrines but a method of investigation.[15] It provided the insight into the dialectic of man's existence which is historical existence.[16]

The essay on demythologizing, which was first delivered as an address to pastors in 1941,[17] precipitated the most heated debate of any of his writings. Actually, the program of interpretation outlined in that essay had been a standard part of Bultmann's method for at least two decades. However, the terminology was so striking that a furor erupted.

Of more importance than the demythologizing essay were several other works of Bultmann. His 1926 book on Jesus [18] is considered a masterpiece by most New Testament scholars. His two-volume *Theology of the New Testament*,[19] also available in English, first appeared in German in 1948 and 1953. His commentary on John's Gospel, now available in English, is considered to be the most outstanding commentary on the Fourth Gospel in this period.[20] In it he interpreted the Gospel against the background of Gnosticism.

In 1925, Bultmann published an essay, "What Sense Is There to Speak of God?" [21] in which he prophetically stressed a number of themes which he later developed in his theology.

In 1963, he published another essay, "The Idea of God and
Modern Man,"[22] as a response to Bishop John A. T. Robinson's *Honest To God*. In this essay, he responded to the contemporary emphases of Robinson's radical talk about God
and to the "death of God" idea.

The essays of the 1920s laid out the major themes which
Bultmann later developed. He worked progressively and
without any radical changes of direction. He saw the weaknesses of liberalism and the advantages which dialectical
theology offered, but he never belonged to either. When his
own students, now the teachers, moved away from some of his
emphases, he showed no disappointment or resentment. His
own pursuit of truth had removed the possibility of his being
affected by wounded pride. His responses to his critics have
been kind and often appreciative. One may differ with his
interpretations and theological conclusions, but one cannot
find fault with his spirit or his intent.

Throughout Bultmann's theological career, he has acknowledged indebtedness to Martin Heidegger with whom he was
closely associated in the late 1920s. From 1923 to 1928
Heidegger was professor of philosophy in Marburg. In 1927
he published his great work *Sein und Zeit*[23] which provided
Bultmann an understanding of existence and a system of concepts which appear in all of his subsequent writings. The
close association between Bultmann and Heidegger was interrupted in 1933 by Heidegger's close relationship with
Hitler's emerging Nazi party,[24] but Bultmann later repeated
his statements of appreciation for Heidegger. Although Heidegger has written in such a way since World War II that he
is referred to as "the later Heidegger," our concern is with
the thought of Heidegger as published in his *Sein und Zeit*.

The theology of Bultmann is biblical in content, Protestant-
Lutheran in background, and dialectical in its immediate
expression, but the indelible imprint of Heidegger's existentialist analysis is obvious throughout. To understand Bultmann's theology one must look first at Heidegger.

II. Bultmann's Understanding of Man - The Concept of Existence

Bultmann considered liberal theology to be in error in that it was concerned with man and not with God, who is the only proper subject of theology.[1] But Bultmann also believed that man cannot know God directly as an entity, since God is not an object. Man can know God only in response to God's revelation, i.e., his Word addressed to man. Hence, man cannot speak of God without speaking of himself at the same time. So, theology becomes a matter of speaking about man's existence as determined by faith in God. Therefore, the starting point for understanding Bultmann's theology is the clarification of the concept of existence.[2]

The basic word is "existence" (*Existenz*) which stresses the particular kind of being of individual man as opposed to the kind of being found in natural objects (*Vorhandenheit*). Only man is existence. Objects are merely extant. A further distinction is made between "existential" and "existentialist." Existential (*das Existentielle*) understanding is the particular individual understanding of existence, or man's understanding of himself in the light of his possibilities. Existentialist (*das Existential*) understanding is the philosophical or analytical understanding of man's existence in the abstract.[3] The existentialist understanding of man deals with the structure of man's existence. The existential understanding is that of the individual as he decides his own existence. His questions

arise existentially. If he analyzes them philosophically, the
analysis is existentialist understanding. This distinction of
Bultmann corresponds to Heidegger's distinction between
"ontological" and "ontic."

BULTMANN AND HEIDEGGER

The content of Bultmann's theology is intensely biblical, and
his own claim is that his whole work of interpretation has
been a radical exposition of the doctrine of justification by
faith. However, he has been obviously influenced by Heidegger's existentialism, and Bultmann has gratefully acknowledged his indebtedness. He considers Heidegger's existentialist analysis of human existence in *Sein und Zeit* the ideal
philosophical approach for theological method. Its understanding of the ontological structure of being is, he feels, a
secularized and independent version of the understanding of
man found in the New Testament.[4] Bultmann's primary theological hermeneutical principle is that man can speak of
nothing except that which he knows in his own existence, and
"that existentialist analysis is simply the systematization of
the self-understanding of existence involved in existence
itself."[5]

Heidegger set out with the deliberate intention of con-
structing an ontology with the fact of existence as the starting
point. He thought such a clarification would be of value in
philosophy. Bultmann welcomed this clarification and applied it to theology.[6]

Bultmann and Heidegger share several basic conceptions
in their writings, of which two are quite important. One is the
importance of the way questions are put (*Fragestellung*).
The other is the system of basic concepts and terminology
used in dealing with the subject matter (*Begrifflichkeit*). The
way a question is put determines to some extent what the
answer will be.[7] Bultmann thinks the interpreter asks questions of the text. For instance, if we take the question "What

is the meaning of death?" we can see the importance of the way the question is put. A philosophy professor contemplates the question in the quietness of his study somewhat abstractly. But suppose the same professor has just been told by his surgeon that he will soon die. Obviously, the question now has a different meaning. The man confronted by death puts the question existentially. Similarly, it makes a great deal of difference what system of concepts one employs. Every discipline has such a set of concepts. Heidegger calls his concepts *"existentialia"* because they are in terms of existentiality.[8]

The analysis begins with Being itself (*Sein*) which is to be distinguished from specific instances of being (*Seiendes*). *Dasein* is Heidegger's term for specifically "human" existence. The word literally means "being there." It stresses man's distinct kind of existence in contrast to objects which are only extant. The analysis of *Dasein* reveals that such existence is at once both subject and object. A subject can look upon himself as an object. Hence, existence is characterized by possibility, or potentiality. This does not mean that human existence is in a state of becoming. Man does not have properties as objects do. Rather, man, who is capable of decision, can achieve or lose his existence.

Individuality is obviously important in the analysis of *Dasein*. Existence does not appear in general, nor is man an example of the universal. Existence occurs only in concrete individual life. Furthermore, individuality is characterized by the first personal pronoun. It is always "my" existence, and "mineness" describes it.[9] Consequently, the emphasis must be on the personal, unique, and individual aspects of human life. General talk about existence objectifies it and hence distorts or destroys it.

Human existence is "being-in-the-world."[10] This term does not specify a location even though all existence is located in the world. The term is understood existentially. It points out that man lives alongside the world (though in it) but remains distinct from it. The world consists of the things which are

at hand and are useful to man. Thus man's understanding of
his own existence is given along with that of his world.[11]

Heidegger distinguishes, and Bultmann agrees, between
two modes of being: authenticity and inauthenticity. Authentic (*eigentlich*) existence occurs when man recognizes that he
has been thrown into the world but chooses to accept the risks
and dangers, and decides to be his own potentiality. Inauthentic (*uneigentlich*) existence occurs when a person loses the
distinction between himself and the world and fails to decide
for his possibilities. The threat of inauthentic existence is
never removed. One must repeatedly choose to be. John
Macquarrie has illustrated this distinction by calling attention to the idea in John's Gospel that Christians are "in" but
"not of" the world. To maintain the distinction is to exist
authentically. To lose the distinction is to exist inauthentically.[12]

In his everyday inauthentic existence, man knows "care"
which is itself constituted by possibility, facticity, and fallenness. Care (*Sorge*) is the burden of inauthentic existence.
When man becomes aware of his being-in-the-world he stands
incomplete before the future. This is "possibility." Man is in
a situation as a result of "thrownness" and is related to that
situation. This is his "facticity." He also learns that not only
is he in the world, but has already surrendered to it. This is
his "fallenness."[13]

Out of the analysis of "care," Heidegger distinguished a
past, present, and future which he called "temporality."[14]
Temporality is thus the "three-fold structure of care."[15] These
terms must not be understood in the strict temporal sense. In
achieving authentic existence one must unite these three. The
past is not merely that which has preceded. Man takes the
past into his existence by accepting its guilt. The future is
more than the "not yet." It is the potentiality toward which
man moves. The present is not just "now." Rather, it is the
situation of responsible decision to include past and future in
authentic existence. Only man has history. Historicity is
therefore another word for human existence.

But human existence is constantly threatened. Macquarrie has summarized Heidegger's discussion in a convenient three-fold way.[16] (1) "Facticity" stresses my stark individualism. I not only have been "thrown" into the world, but I am and I have to be. I am already a fact and never get to start from the beginning. Being-in-the-world is always individual existence among the things of the world. (2) "Depersonalization" is the form of the threat issuing from being-in-the-world with others. I am also a being-with-others and must not regard them as things, but as existing selves. If I see others as objects, the crowd, the herd, the "they," or the "public," I succumb to the threat of depersonalization. Heidegger's radical individualism must be seen against the background of a world depersonalized by industrialization and totalitarian states. (3) "Fallenness" is the kind of inauthentic existence in which one has lost himself in the world. In fallenness (not from some original righteousness) man is repeatedly tempted to fall into the world, is tranquillized so that he no longer is sensitive to the demands of existential living, and is alienated from his true self to the degree that he gets entangled with himself.[17]

Death[18] is an important concept in both Heidegger and Bultmann. The concern is not with the general question of death, but rather with the existential understanding of my own death. Although I may learn from the death of others, I achieve a wholeness in my existence by my own awareness and anticipation of death. Death is not simply the end. Rather, death is that being-in-the-world-no-more. If I confront the possibility of death, I sense the meaning of isolation which results from being cut off from the world and from others. Such existential understanding of death sets existence in a clearer light. Man is a being-toward-death.

THE GREEK AND BIBLICAL VIEWS OF MAN

We have noted that Bultmann's theology depends heavily on his interpretation of human existence. Inasmuch as Greek thinking permeates the thought of Western man, Bultmann was obliged to show how biblical thought differed from Greek thought. It is his contention that the existentialist understanding of man's existence is in keeping with that of biblical faith and is therefore ideal for interpreting biblical faith.

His preference for the biblical understanding over that of Greek philosophy is obvious in all of his writings, but a number of his essays are of particular importance. In 1930 he published "The Historicity of Man and Faith," [19] in which he presented his plan for interpreting man in terms of Heidegger's analysis of existence. In 1940 he published "The Understanding of Man and the World in the New Testament and in the Greek World," [20] in which he contrasted the Greek view of man with that of the New Testament. Other essays which contribute to this theme are "The Significance of the Old Testament for the Christian Faith," [21] and "The Idea of God and Modern Man." [22] His Gifford Lectures [23] of 1955 are exceedingly important for the understanding of man.

The Greeks, according to Bultmann, saw man as an instance of the general rather than as an individual, particular man. They viewed the world (cosmos) as a harmonious whole with man an integral part, and they understood the true nature of dichotomous man as spirit. [24]

In his primitive existence, man lived in fear of the demonic forces, but he found security in the community of city life. Thus, he came to understand himself in terms of the city, and emphasized his community nature more than his individual nature. For instance, the individual would freely give up his own life for the life of his city. His own position and dignity, therefore, depended upon his membership in the city. In time, the Greeks divinized this order of life and related it to the divine beings in the realm above. However, their progress in science enabled them to recognize that they had constructed this order which they had divinized. When this happened, they did not abandon the gods, even though the gods had lost their authority. In replacing religion, science retained a kind of theological outlook—the Greeks saw their own earthly order as related to a universal order which was the "real" world above. Man was a part of the general world.

The world was seen as a unity in which gods, men, and things existed in a harmonious whole. The world was interpreted by analogy as a work of art. Consequently, man saw himself as a part of this cosmos, and he worked to fit himself into its complex unity. He came to see himself as one object among the others, a particular example of the general. The rational description of this closed coherent system became a world view (*Weltanschauung*). It included even the gods. In such a system, man understands himself as secure. He is safeguarded by the whole. Individual existence consists of conformity to the whole.

Although man was dichotomous, body and spirit, his real existence was ideal or eternal. As spirit imprisoned in a body, he saw the true meaning of life in the real transcendent world. Consequently, the threats of this life lost their meaning. Even death posed no threat since it was but an episode in life. Man's true existence was beyond the temporal in the realm of timelessness.

The biblical understanding of man is radically different. There are no gods conveniently harmonized with the world and at man's disposal. In the biblical understanding of existence, there is one God who is no part of the world but stands apart, calling man into question. Even though God may be concerned for all of his creatures, including the sparrows, he is the Creator who stands in lordship over men. He does not answer to man's questions or reason.

Biblical faith knows no comfortable secure world view. Its unity is not guaranteed by some ideal world above. This world is the "real" world. Man is part of the world. The world threatens man in that he can lose his own true existence and become merely an object of the world. God is not a part of the world but stands above it. Man is in the world but responsible to God. He achieves his true existence only by his individual decisions and not by integration into the cosmos. The Christian understanding of existence actually accomplishes a kind of "detachment from the world" to which Bultmann alludes in his discussions of 1 Corinthians 7:29–31. Paul admonished the Corinthian Christians to live in the world "as though not." This world is passing away and men of faith must be freed from the world's snares so that they can belong to God (Rom. 14:8).

In both the Old and New Testaments,[25] man is individual man, in sharp contrast to man in Greek thought. Man has no guarantee which allows him to get lost in the crowd. He stands naked as an isolated individual hearing the Word of God calling him to decision. No comfortable world view exists to free him from his responsibility. In his day-to-day historical existence he stands before God. He is not true spirit imprisoned in a body, but a historical existence, a unity. Death is no escape for him, nor is his salvation inevitable and automatic. He is an individual man who must choose to be responsible to God.

Man is historical. He has been thrown into the world which he did not choose. He already has a past for which he is responsible, and its guilt is a part of his own personal existence. God confronts him and demands that he love his neighbor.[26] In every "now," man is called to abandon his past and live the future in dependence on God. This historical encounter with God's Word calling him into the future brings out man's sin. In dread, man cringes before his responsibility for the future and thereby rejects God, or he mistakenly tries to develop his own kind of righteousness before God and falls into pride, again rejecting God.[27]

In the New Testament, man's salvation comes as a liberation from sin which held him to his past. Forgiveness destroys the hold of the past so that man can be open to God's future. Such forgiveness is grounded in the event of Jesus Christ [28] and makes man free to be himself in this world "as though not" in this world.

In response to the question "Greece or Christianity?" Bultmann concluded[29] that a Christian must forever choose his historical existence in each moment of existence and must not lean on the Greek explanation of existence. This does not make Christianity a foe of the secular, because it is precisely in this world that man is confronted by the Word of God calling him to authentic existence. Authentic existence is not asceticism. Christian faith seeks no shelter for its eschatological community. Rather, it demands that by faith one must live eschatologically in this world.

PREVIEW OF BULTMANN'S UNDERSTANDING OF EXISTENCE

The discussion of Heidegger's analysis of existence, with which Bultmann agrees, and the presentation of Bultmann's contrast between Greek and biblical views of man indicate a number of key terms which will appear throughout this study. Although some of them will receive detailed discussion later, it may help to define briefly some of these descriptive terms of human existence.

Human existence is, first of all, existence under the demand of God the Creator. Although God is known and discussed only on the basis of encounter with him in response to his Word, he stands as the determining presupposition for all of Bultmann's theology. Every thought of man is intelligible only in the light of his belonging to God and being "subject to the claim of God."[30] Bultmann shares the view of God characteristic of the dialectical theologians. He stresses God's "otherness" and "holiness." He continually points out that man's creatureliness is reflected in the awareness that he does not have the world "at his disposal"[31] and that God constantly calls him into question.[32]

Since man knows God only in human existence, it is not surprising that one finds it difficult to separate Bultmann's view of God from the discussion of human existence. Nevertheless, Bultmann wrote an essay, "Faith in God the Creator," in which he stressed that by faith in God the Creator, man learns of his own nothingness, that he is bound, that life is not at his disposal but at the Creator's disposal.[33] Furthermore, to "know" God as Creator is not to have concepts about him but to acknowledge him as Creator, and to submit to him so as to be determined by him.[34] The very mention of God as Creator is to say that God is over against the world in such a way as to stress the distinctive difference.[35] When accused of reducing God to being only in man's subjective experience, Bultmann denied the validity of the accusation.[36] It is true that he denies that man can know God objectively, but his whole theology rests on the conviction that God, Who Is, acted redemptively in Jesus Christ.

Human existence is "worldly" existence. To Heidegger, human existence is being-in-the-world, and man receives his understanding of the world from its usefulness to him. Bultmann, following John and Paul, views the world not in the scientific but in the existential sense. In contrast to Greek thought, in which the real world was elsewhere, Bultmann understands the biblical writers to speak of this world as the real world. It is the historical world. Bultmann understands man not in terms of origin, or even destiny, but in terms of genuine existence in this world.

Human existence is always historical. Only man is historical, and this is so clearly his nature that human existence is the same as historicity. This means that man should not be viewed as a substance or as an object of nature. In biblical faith man is always understood as standing in the world with a past and challenged by the promise of the future. Things happen to man. Man responds in his freedom. By responding in his own history, man achieves existence. If we impose our way of thinking, which is Greek in origin, on the New Testament, we distort that message. Then, the world becomes a place in which man stands alongside other objects as a "what," but in the New Testament this is not the case.[37] Historical understanding is the true understanding of man's

existence, and only in these terms can man understand the
Christian message.

Historicity stresses not only the "happenedness" of man
but that man is at the mercy of history. His previous decisions
and actions have already become his history. He did not get
to choose his generation, nationality, or human situation, but
he is required to choose his own history. To be a man is precisely existence in this situation.[38] Historicity means that each
man is responsible for his own personal history. It is always
his own concrete worldly existence, and his own personal response means more than the accidental contingencies of the
historical setting.[39]

Historical existence with its demand for decision opens the
door for man to choose God and authenticity. Consequently,
human existence is potentiality-to-be. Existence is always
standing before the future, not in the durative but in the punctiliar sense. In every moment of decision man either chooses
existence as determined by God, or existence determined by
sin.

Possibility endows human life with uniqueness. Heidegger
considered this possibility open to any man who would choose
authenticity,[40] but Bultmann interprets human existence under
the power of sin so that only by faith in Christ does man
choose authenticity. Only by faith in Christ and in Christian
love for fellowman has man come to this authentic realization
of existence.[41]

Potentiality-to-be applies to society as it does to individuals. In biblical faith, just as individuals gain authentic existence only by response to God's call, so in historical encounters
people are constituted as the people of God.[42]

Human existence is basically individual. Bultmann's understanding of existence is individualistic. Man never exists in
general, but always as individual, concrete, historical man.
Therefore, it is really possible to talk about God only in the
first person singular. This is the reason existence is described
as "mine," rather than even as "ours."

Existence is therefore determined by a person's decisions in any given moment. Existence is punctiliar rather than linear. In Bultmann's view of man, there is no continuing state or process upon which one can presume. In every moment the person stands in history confronted by the future with the demand and the Word of God. He achieves and reclaims authentic existence only in these decisions. Inauthentic existence results if he fails to choose or chooses incorrectly.

III. Bultmann's Understanding of History

Christian faith is inseparably related to the historical person of Jesus Christ and to the New Testament documents which report that event. The primary task of interpretation is bridging the time gap between that history and man's present understanding. So, the problem of understanding history is central in the task of interpretation. Some think that this is *the* problem which has consumed more of Bultmann's interest than any other.[1]

HISTORIE, GESCHICHTE, ESCHATOLOGY, AND HISTORICITY

There are four words which appear to be the foci of Bultmann's view of history: *Historie, Geschichte*, eschatology, and historicity.

It is unfortunate that English has no convenient way of translating the two German words for history, *Historie* and *Geschichte*, which are basic to understanding Bultmann. In spite of some uncertainty, the distinction appears to date from Martin Kähler (1892).[2] *Historie* designates what actually happened. It points to those events which take place in the cause-effect chain and which can be studied by historians employing scientific methods. The corresponding adjective "historical" (*historisch*) is used about a person who existed or an event which really happened and can be described in the terms of historical research. For instance, the historical Jesus would be Jesus as he actually was and can be studied in scientific historical research. Bultmann is not curious about the historical Jesus, but is profoundly concerned with the Christ event.

By contrast, *Geschichte* designates an event of history which continues to have influence or meaning on later persons and events. It deals with the encounter of persons,[3] and its emphasis is on the personal meaning of event, or existential history. The cognate adjective *geschichtlich* is now translated in English by the word "historic."[4] To Bultmann, the "historical" (*historisch*) Jesus would be Jesus who could be known objectively by the historians' critical method of study. The "historic" (*geschichtlich*) Christ, however, is the Christ who has existential meaning today as he confronts man through the proclamation of the kerygma. Bultmann's purpose in emphasizing the "historic" Christ is based on his conviction that God speaks to man through this message. The "historical" Jesus could be the object of research even for the merely curious, but the "historic" Christ is not an object of research for the curious but of vital interest to faith.

Consequently, Bultmann, who is a competent historian in the scientific sense, rejects *Historie* as the basis for faith and contends that Christian faith is grounded in the "historic" event of Christ. The basic reason is that he really believes God spoke and speaks now to man through the proclamation of the Christ event. However, there are other supporting reasons which are derived from his understanding of *Historie*. He maintains that all purely historical knowledge is (1) ambiguous, (2) relative, and (3) a closed sequence of cause and effect which leaves no room for any unique elements.[5] The ambiguity is obvious in that the "lives" of Jesus as reconstructed are constantly changing.[6] The relative nature of the historical is obvious in that all events are seen only as they fall into the proper categories. Nothing unique can be considered, and this fact severely limits the kind of history with which theologians are dealing. The "closed" cause and effect idea which is normative in *Historie* leaves no room for any act of God, or else would reduce God to a cause.

Faith is related to the historic Christ of the proclamation. This kind of history (*Geschichte*) speaks existentially to man, and he understands himself in his own encounter with such events.

The term "eschatology" literally means "last things." When defined in the context of history as *Historie*, it means the end of history. However, the end of history means not only its termination, but its goal or purpose—teleology. In Jewish apocalyptic literature, eschatology was seen as the end of history brought about dramatically by the action of God. When eschatology is defined in the context of history as *Geschichte*, the meaning is not necessarily a future termination, but rather a realization of authentic existence in the present. Although Bultmann acknowledges that the New Testament contains the Judaistic apocalyptic eschatology as well as the present-tense eschatology found in such statements of John as "I am the resurrection," Bultmann strongly favors the understanding of Christ as the great eschatological event, and existence in faith as eschatological existence now.

The eschatological understanding of history is undeniably important in the New Testament, as indicated by interpreters such as Albert Schweitzer and Johannes Weiss. The Jewish apocalyptic eschatological views such as are found in Daniel are also repeated in the New Testament. Bultmann's existential interpretation of such apocalyptic eschatology amounts to demythologizing it. He certainly does not take it literally, nor even as future. However, in spite of the language which includes clouds, angels, trumpet sounds, and other dramatic clothing, it amounts to the urgent call of God to eschatological living now. When such eschatology loses its futurity, and is known existentially, it becomes "historic" existence.

By using the term "historicity," which is identical in mean-

ing with "existence," and "self-understanding,"[7] Bultmann
stresses the radical nature of man's existence as a fact only in
the entanglements of history. Man is at the mercy of history.[8]
He does not pass through history, nor does he observe and
investigate it. He is "nothing but history," a being to whom
"things happen."[9] Not only is he delivered over to history,[10]
but he realizes his existence only within history. Such meaning is always present as man awakens to each moment by
decisions for eschatological existence now.

To be sure, historicity stresses that man is thrown into
history with numerous limitations and liabilities over which
he has no control. But, it also means that he has personal,
individual history in which he casts many important and
deciding votes. He lives a concrete life in the actual world
and partakes of the accidents and ambiguities of *Historie*,
but, as man, he decides his own personal history and becomes
"historic." Historicity is *Geschichtlichkeit*, existence with
authentic meaning.

THE NATURE AND MEANING OF HISTORY

In prehistoric times, people told myths because they had no
real history.[11] When man developed nations, he also developed historical narratives. In Greek thought, history was understood by analogy with the seasons of nature and with
cosmic movements, which gave rise to the idea of cyclic history, and made history analogous to natural science—all
events would happen again. The periods or cycles of history
were both rationalized and later historicized.[12] For instance,
ages were schemed out in sequence denoted by the metals,
gold, silver, bronze, and iron as in Daniel.[13]

Old Testament thought was determined by theology, and
consequently history was the actual deeds of men who were
understood in terms of God. History was not seen by analogy
with nature but in terms of man's response to the judgment of
God. Jewish apocalyptic literature dropped the idea of resto-
ration as found in the cyclic view and added the eschatologi-

cal view. In later Judaism, human destiny replaced the
destiny of the world and the two ages replaced the cyclical
periods. Apocalypticism believed that the old age would be
brought to an end by God's judgment.[14]

In the New Testament both views, the Old Testament view
of history and the apocalyptic view, appear, but the apocalyptic view prevails.[15] The event of Christ is not a historical
event like that of Moses which people look back upon. Rather, the event of Christ is the eschatological event. It brings
the old age to a close. The Christian community understands
itself not as historical but as eschatological. It belongs to a
new age.[16] But the Christians expected Christ to return soon
and bring the apocalyptic conclusion. When he did not do so,
eschatology became a problem. The young church became a
religion and became interested in tradition, eye witnesses,
and doctrines.

Paul's understanding of history was determined by his
eschatology. Paul saw Israel's history not as cycles of sin and
forgiveness but as a unity. The unity included all mankind in
Adam brought to fulfillment in Moses.[17] All men, Jews and
Gentiles, are under God's judgment (Rom. 3:19), so the end
of history will come not as a result of historical development
but as a breaking off, by an act of God. So, to Paul, meaning
in history would have to be meaning given to it by God and
not that evident within history. Therefore, Bultmann maintains that Paul stressed man's historicity,[18] which, in fact,
shows that Paul's view was an existentialist interpretation.
Man is there, in-the-world, and becomes what he is through
decisions. Man lives before God and his life is authentic or
counterfeit as determined by God's approval or disapproval.
Paul also retained, however, the future aspect of eschatology
which John completely gave up for a present idea of eschatological existence.

The failure of the parousia-hope led the church to consider
its history, which led to the origin of a world history in the
strict sense.[19] In this view, Christ was central. All prior events
were preparatory. All subsequent events became a continuing

sequence of events in this world. Meaning in history came to
be seen not as in the Old Testament in which every event had
meaning, but as a meaning imposed by God as history moved
toward its goal. Within this idea of history, individual history
arose in the discussion of man's freedom of will.

The teleological view of history was secularized in later
thought. For instance, Kant secularized Christian teleology.
Bultmann thinks that all of these miss the point of history.

He likewise rejects the historicism of the past century in
which history was treated causally and came to be regarded
as a science of facts. Historians appeared to think that they
could stand above, or apart from, history and appraise it
objectively. Bultmann thinks that history is about man.

R. G. Collingwood [20] spoke in a way that Bultmann appre-
ciated. He understood history as the "actions of human beings" which were done in the past. Collingwood argued that
the historian must always study the previous actions of men
from the inside, as it were, re-creating them in the thought
process. [21] This kind of historical research would also be self-
knowledge. It would not require surrender of the author, but
would involve a critical rethinking of the event. Whereas a
natural scientist looks upon his evidence as object and himself
as the subject, the historian has a different approach. Historical knowledge, if it makes any difference, is existential knowledge. [22]

Bultmann's understanding of history is especially clear in
his interpretation of historical documents. Schleiermacher
had pointed out that philological interpretation was inadequate, and that the interpreter had to reproduce within himself the situation about which the text spoke. Dilthey had followed Schleiermacher along this line, but Bultmann developed the idea under the term "preunderstanding." Bultmann
believes that interpretation of historical texts is possible only
because author and interpreter live in and share the same
historical world. The interpreter goes to the text with a pre-
understanding, and therefore he asks questions of the text. It
would seem that such an interpreter could "know" only sub-

jective matter, and that an objective historical situation could not be known. However, Bultmann concedes that we can know some objective historical events, but never the whole event, and that such events are hardly worth investigation. Bare facts are not important, or are important only in that they convey meaning to the interpreter. Historical research is not like scientific research. The historian does have an interest. He encounters history existentially, and he must reenact the event in his understanding of it. So, "the object of historical knowledge is man himself in his subjective nature." [23]

The historian does not assign a meaning to history or to its events. Events have meanings which they disclose to man. Therefore, man cannot say what is *the* meaning of history, since he cannot see the end of history. But in individual historicity there is the possibility that events and epochs have meaning.

In summary, Bultmann sees history in terms of personal, individual encounter. Historical knowledge comes through encounter with history in decisive moments. Historical events have their own meaning within themselves. There is no knowledge of history apart from engagement in it. It is impossible to speak of an overall meaning of history, but this does not mean that it is meaningless or absurd. Bultmann means that one cannot stand outside of it and observe it. He does not discount the meaning in history, but he certainly minimizes its importance for faith. Faith is man's response to God's Word spoken to man and, of course, encountered by man in history.[24] So faith and history are related, but faith is not dependent upon historical validation. Christianity is historical and its ground is a historical event, but this history does not guarantee faith. Faith abandons all human efforts to guarantee it by logic, history, or works, and is a direct act of dependence on God and an openness to God's future.

Such faith as obedient self-commitment resulting in a kind of detachment from the world appears to be possible only "when it is faith in Jesus Christ." [25]

IV. Bultmann and the Historical Jesus

Bultmann's distinction between *Historie* and *Geschichte* is in evidence in his response to the "quest" of the "historical Jesus."[1] In all of his writings, even from the earliest essays to the present, Bultmann repeats the refrain that Christian faith is not dependent on the historical Jesus but on the Christ event. He has consistently maintained that it is impossible to write a modern biography of Jesus because the source material (the Gospels) is confessional rather than biographical or historical. However, Bultmann does not regret this limitation. He maintains that we do not need to know the historical Jesus.

Sören Kierkegaard had made a similar statement a century earlier, that faith did not depend upon the historical information about Jesus. He said that if the first-century Christians had left us only the assertion that God had appeared in the servant Jesus, who had lived, taught, and died, it would have been adequate.[2]

To my knowledge, no New Testament scholar denies the fact that Jesus lived. Bultmann certainly does not. The term "historical Jesus" has nothing to do with the question about Jesus' historicity. Not only is this fact assumed, but Bultmann also concedes that there is a continuity between Jesus and the Christ proclaimed in the Christian preaching. However, he continues to maintain that the attempt to write a "historical" account of Jesus as he really was, separate from the faith men placed in him, is not only impossible, but also illegitimate and useless.

Such a historical Jesus would be Jesus in terms of modern scientific historical research. It would imply technically that certain facts had been established by scholarship as true.[3] It is quite obvious, and stated by Bultmann, that the term "Christ of faith" presupposes *that* Jesus lived, taught, and died. However, the only sources we have are the Gospels, and in them Christ was presented as the one in whom the disciples believed. He was Lord and Savior. They were interested not in scientific *Historie*, but rather in the great event as an event of *Geschichte*, which had profound meaning for their lives.

THE QUEST OF THE HISTORICAL JESUS

During the eighteenth and nineteenth centuries, scholars wrote numerous biographies of Jesus. Many factors encouraged the endeavor, not the least of which was a sincere regard for knowledge of Jesus. However, the new factor which contributed most to this phenomenon was the rise of scientific historical methods. Biblical scholars believed that they now had the tools to accomplish the task they had always wanted to do— discover Jesus as he really was. These "lives" of Jesus constituted a theological movement of significance. The more outstanding biographies of this undertaking were summarized and evaluated by Albert Schweitzer in the classic volume *The Quest of the Historical Jesus*.[4] Schweitzer concluded that the "quest" was a failure, in that the portraits of Jesus resembled the biographers more than they resembled one another. It is generally agreed that this volume marked the end of the "old" quest.

The quest was conducted by historians who were under the influence of a developing scientific understanding of nature, in which nature was considered a closed system. History came to be seen in terms of nature. In fact, history and nature together appeared to comprise all of reality.[5] It is obvious why

Bultmann would reject this view of history which was basic to the quest. A reevaluation of the method of historical research has led to the recognition of history's relativity, and the consequent acknowledgment that the "historical Jesus" was not "Jesus as he actually was" but the "historians' Jesus." [6]

Liberal theologians who engaged in this quest also were under the impression that Jesus impressed people because of his personality, and they sought to understand this great personality. This understanding produced a "liberal Jesus" who was the example and aim of Christian living. Adolf Harnack portrayed this Jesus in popular theological form in his *What Is Christianity?* The songs of the period reflect the sentimental attachment to the great and impressive personality. Popular novels such as Charles M. Sheldon's *In His Steps* [7] popularized this Jesus, and convinced people that they had come to know him as he really was.

REJECTION OF THE QUEST OF
THE HISTORICAL JESUS

Martin Kähler published a significant volume on this subject in 1896 entitled *The So-Called Historical Jesus and the Historic, Biblical Christ.* [8] He rejected the "Life of Jesus" movement on the grounds that the sources were inadequate for historical purposes. The Gospels were adequate for faith but completely lacking in the kind of information needed for writing a personality sketch of Jesus, and the attempts to psychoanalyze Jesus were completely wrong. Kähler asked, why make such an attempt when we already have adequate reason to believe in Jesus and to receive the forgiveness of our sins? To the reply that scholars were just taking the humanity of Jesus seriously, Kähler responded that instead they were antagonistic to Christology. The focus of faith is rather the confession of the disciples that "Jesus is Lord." They knew the historical Jesus but were left weak and defeated by his death. However, after the resurrection they were of a different stripe. They went out preaching the gospel of salvation by faith, not founding schools which taught the teachings of Jesus. Christ called forth faith, and the preaching was about this Christ.

While Kähler did not consistently distinguish between *Historie* and *Geschichte*, as does Bultmann, he made the basic distinction. He also saw the historical Jesus as the object of historical-critical research, and not the same as Jesus. This historical Jesus he regarded as irrelevant for faith. He also considered the historic Christ as the object of faith. His objection was not to the historical-critical method as such, only to its application to the effort to write an analysis of Jesus from documents which dealt primarily with faith. Kähler was motivated by the desire to keep Christian faith understandable to laymen, and the historical studies seemed to say that faith was dependent upon the complicated research of professional historians.

The influence of Kähler on Bultmann is clear. In 1929 Bultmann wrote "The Significance of the Historical Jesus for the Theology of Paul," [9] in which he argued that Paul was not directly influenced by the historical Jesus and did not proclaim him. Bultmann has consistently rejected this quest, and when some of his own former students opened the "New Quest of the Historical Jesus," [10] Bultmann declined to join the searching party. [11]

Two outstanding factors explain Bultmann's rejection of the quest for the historical Jesus: (1) the failure of the old quest, and (2) the unsuitable nature of the sources.

The old quest had failed. It had proceeded on the basis of an unacceptable view of history and had operated on an incorrect understanding of the nature of the source material. The focus of the quest had been the personality of Jesus, an emphasis which itself indicated that the searchers thought that it was Jesus' personality which impressed people. The great variety of results which were obtained further convinced Bultmann of the futility of the quest.

Bultmann's appraisal of the New Testament sources would further preclude such a quest. Bultmann thinks that the Gospels, the only sources for such a study, are faith documents constructed by editors within the early church. He also thinks that by the time the Gospels were written, the historical figure of Jesus had already been covered over with pagan mythology, so that Jesus was seen as a preexistent being.[12] We have noted how important the *Sitz im Leben*, the life situation, was in shaping the documents. If that setting was in the Hellenistic rather than the Jewish community, then the greater distance would certainly suggest more distortion. In 1926, Bultmann wrote,

> I do indeed think that we can now know almost nothing concerning the life and personality of Jesus, since the early Christian sources show no interest in either, are moreover fragmentary and often legendary; and other sources about Jesus do not exist.[13]

The method of form criticism has some presuppositions which figure prominently in Bultmann's treatment of the Gospel contents. Again, at this point he appears to be indebted to Martin Kähler.[14] His *History of the Synoptic Tradition*[15] is an outstanding example of this method.

Of greatest significance in Bultmann's understanding of the historical Jesus are two theological factors. (1) He thinks that the theology of the New Testament deals with the Christ of the kerygma and not with the historical Jesus. (2) He thinks that the nature of faith makes the historical Jesus irrelevant.

The theology of the New Testament, largely from Paul and John, deals with Christ of the kerygma and not with the historical Jesus. Paul was not influenced by the historical Jesus directly or indirectly.[16] He based his claim to apostolic authority (Gal. 1:12–17) not upon his knowledge of or acquaintance with the historical Jesus but upon an appearance of the risen Lord. In all of his writings, he claimed the authority of Jesus' teaching in only two instances (1 Cor. 7:10f.; 1 Cor. 9:14), and these are not crucial for faith. Paul preached that Jesus had come, died, and had been raised. This was the proclamation he had heard, and he was thereby forced to decide whether he would acknowledge that God had acted redemptively in this event. When he decided to acknowledge Christ, he proclaimed what he had heard, which was neither Jesus' own teachings nor information about him, but rather *that* the event had happened and that it was God's saving act. Jesus was not a teacher with a new concept of God, nor a hero or an example.[17] The cross was not a symbol but a naked fact of history, in which it was claimed God's judgment and salvation came to man.

In like manner, Christ confronts men *only* in the proclamation of this gospel. This gospel is not composed of universal truths or timeless ideas, but is a historical fact.[18] The kerygma was the beginning of faith and of New Testament theology. There was no "Christian" faith before it. Therefore, the teachings of Jesus are a part of Judaism,[19] not Christianity.[20] To put it another way, a complete historical knowledge of Jesus' teachings and deeds would not be the kerygma, or the occasion of faith. Jesus' message is therefore the presupposition of theology in the New Testament. Christian faith becomes possible only when the Christian kerygma proclaims that the Crucified and Risen One was the event of salvation.

Whereas Jesus had proclaimed the kingdom of God as future, Paul preached that it had happened in the event of Christ, a past event. In like manner, the Christian proclamation was not a systematic exposition of Jesus' teachings or concepts but a proclamation *that* God had acted redemptively in him.[21]

The nature of faith makes the historical Jesus irrelevant, since faith is not assent to doctrine or mastery of historical information. Faith is never validated by historical research,[22] but is always a contemporary[23] existential encounter in which I, confronted by the claim of God in the proclaimed Word, decide to acknowledge Christ. This response of faith is itself a part of the saving event, just as the proclamation of it is a part of the event. To seek validation "behind" the kerygma is to deny its power and to deny faith itself.[24]

Some of the "new questers," working on different premises than the old quest, have thought Bultmann denied the continuity between Jesus and his Christ of faith. Bultmann responded that, of course, there is continuity, since the "kerygma presupposes the historical Jesus,"[25] but he still insists that the Christ of the kerygma is not a historical figure, ascertainable by historical research, so he could not enjoy the kind of continuity being sought.

V. Demythologizing –
Existentialist Interpretation

On April 21, 1941, Bultmann spoke to the pastors of the Confessing Church in Frankfort, Germany, on the subject of demythologizing. His intent was to stress the necessity of proclaiming the gospel of Christ in terms of the modern understanding of men. He was attempting to keep that Confessing Church from being reactionary under the great stress of the war and reverting to some kind of "former" theological stance. His lecture was published later in that same year under the title "New Testament and Mythology." [1] The strange thing about this article is that, even though it has been so revolutionary for the rest of the theological community, it was no new departure for Bultmann. He had been teaching and publishing along this line for the previous twenty years, [2] and one might correctly state that his entire life has been given over to this task.

The essay on demythologizing supplied the most characteristic identifying term for Bultmann and this is rather unfortunate for at least two reasons. The English connotation of the word has suggested to many that Bultmann intended to subtract or eliminate something from the New Testament, but such would be inconceivable to Bultmann. In the light of this misunderstanding, many people have misunderstood the rest of Bultmann's theology, or even worse, have refused to listen to him any further. Many have overlooked the other major contributions of Bultmann for the theological discussion of the present era.

The genius and thoroughness of the man can be easily demonstrated by comparing his original essay with his later publication on the subject—his Shaffer Lectures delivered at Yale University Divinity School in 1951.[3]

THE NATURE OF MYTH

Bultmann's demythologizing depends upon his particular understanding of myth. There are several ways of looking at myth, and some have criticized Bultmann for his particular view. However, he makes no defense of his definition other than to point out that it is the view advocated by the scholars of the History of Religions School, of which he was a product and to which he contributed.

Bultmann defined the nature of myth in terms of its purpose, which was not that of presenting an objective view of the world to be taken literally as if scientific, regardless of what man in the biblical period may have believed about the world. Its purpose was to express man's own understanding of himself in the world in which he lived.[4] Bultmann believes that man, then and now, is primarily concerned about the nature of his own existence in the world, and this conviction for Bultmann is determinative. Consequently, the purpose of myth in the New Testament was to express man's convictions that (1) the origin and purpose of the world are to be found not in the world but beyond it; (2) man "is not lord of his own being" since he is dependent not only on the visible world but also on invisible and mysterious powers; (3) man can be delivered from those powers.[5]

Consequently, Bultmann understands mythology to be man's way of talking about God in human terms, or about the other world in this-worldly terms. In myth, man speaks about the other side (the beyond) in terms of this side. Hence the idea of the transcendence of God is discussed in spatial terms as "above," or "beyond." [6] In the 1951 lectures, Bultmann reaffirmed that "myths speak about gods and demons as powers on which man knows himself to be dependent," and that man "is not master of the world and his life" but rather lives in a world full of mystery and riddles. By using myth, man speaks of these other-worldly powers in the tangible terms of this world, and in the process gives objective reality to them. It goes without saying that Bultmann considers this of primary importance, since the mythology portrays a "certain understanding of human existence." [7]

PRESUPPOSITIONS OF BULTMANN

Bultmann's starting point is a profound conviction that God really is, that he revealed himself in Jesus Christ, that his Word which comes to us through the Bible really is his Word to men, thus calling them to their genuine authentic existence. If Bultmann did not believe that Jesus Christ was unique, then the present discussion would amount to nothing more than a lesson in ancient literature, but he believes differently. He thinks that man has not achieved this authentic existence, the life of faith, in any other way than by faith in Christ. Inasmuch as the written source of our knowledge is the New Testament, its interpretation is of the utmost importance, since only by hearing its proclamation can one respond to God in faith.

But Bultmann believes that this proclamation (kerygma) of the New Testament has come to us in the mythological world view and terminology of the New Testament era, which is not only obsolete but is also impossible for modern scientific man to accept. The writers of the New Testament understood the world to have a three-story construction. The earth was like a saucer with heaven above and hell beneath. The angels and gods (or God) from above and the demons and Satan from below mingled on earth with men and each other, thereby determining man's destiny. Man was subject both to

the good and evil influences of these beings. They could inhabit
a man and make him sick. They could put evil thoughts into
his mind and thus lead him to ruin. The Christian message
(kerygma) stated the convictions that in Jesus Christ God
had sent to earth his preexistent Son, who had died on the
cross to atone for men's sins and had been raised from the
dead. These events began the cosmic catastrophe which was
expected and thereby defeated death and the demonic powers.
Christ was the victor and the end would come shortly.

But modern man has inherited a world view determined
more by science than by such mythology. Bultmann believes
that modern man cannot understand such mythology, much
less accept it. The contemporary view of the world sees nature
and history as closed. That is to say that nature has an observable cause-and-effect sequence which is the very foundation of
life and responsibility. Myth is the expression that outside
powers interfere with this normal cycle, but Bultmann believes
this is incorrect. The problem is unusually acute for the biblical interpreter. Responsible ethical decisions are made on the
basis of believing that human actions are important and have
consequences, and that responsible decisions can be trusted.
To allow for outside powers to intervene would contradict the
foundation upon which responsible decisions are made. But
more acute is the problem posed by Bultmann's conviction
that only by faith in Christ can man really have authentic
existence; but the message of that hope comes in a mythological terminology and framework which obscures the message
for modern man.

Bultmann argues that mythological language is incredible
to modern man, who would be required to sacrifice his intel-
lect to believe it. Scientific knowledge of and mastery of the
world makes the mythological view untenable. Understanding
of nature makes belief in evil spirits no longer acceptable.[8]
Along with this understanding, Bultmann rejects the miracles
of the New Testament with the observation that a modern
man's attempt to explain their historicity by appealing, for

instance, to modern understanding of nervous disorders merely underlines the fact. He further points out that the eschatological expectation framed in this mythological thought did not come about as expected, and therefore we are compelled to dismiss it or seek to understand it in some other way.[9]

Not only has modern science challenged the mythological view, but modern man's understanding of his own existence has demanded a new interpretation. Bultmann sees this as involving such notions that death is the penalty for sinning, that sins could be atoned for by the blood of a sacrifice, and that the resurrection of Jesus (resuscitation of a corpse) could unleash supernatural power for man's life.

Even the course of history has refuted the mythological concepts. The kingdom of God did not come as portrayed in the eschatological mythological drama. History and science do not allow for their perforation by supernatural powers.[10]

BULTMANN'S PROPOSAL

Bultmann's solution is demythologizing, which is the same as existentialist interpretation.

Bultmann's first insistence is that demythologizing is not subtracting or eliminating part of the New Testament.[11] He refuses this temptation and insists that one must either retain or reject the mythological in its entirety. While he may have indicated in his study of the Gospels and the traditions behind them that much material is legendary, he definitely does not mean to subtract it. That is a part of the kerygma which he is seeking to understand. It is Bultmann's contention that the entire kerygma has come to us intertwined with the mythological. The two cannot be separated, and should not be. But mythology must be interpreted. Demythologizing is a hermeneutical method, a method of interpreting the text.

Bultmann's rationale for his program of demythologizing includes his argument that there have been previous attempts in interpretation which were similar to his own. The New

Testament itself invites it, in that it presents numerous contradictory situations—such as Christ's virgin birth and preexist-
ence, the doctrine of creation, and the idea that there are
"rulers of this world" (1 Cor. 2:6ff.) and a "god of this
world" (2 Cor. 4:4). Bultmann notes that throughout the
New Testament there is the idea that human life is controlled
by cosmic forces, but that man is forever challenged to responsible decision as if he determined his own destiny.[12] He
also cites the ancient allegorical method of interpretation,
modern liberalism, and the History of Religions School as
examples of interpretation which unsuccessfully dealt with
the problem of myth and interpretation.

The only solution for Bultmann is existentialist interpretation. Having acknowledged that the New Testament includes
the mythologies of Jewish apocalyptic and Gnostic redemption religions, Bultmann concludes that beneath these layers
there was a basic understanding of human existence. He thinks
that along the lines of Heidegger's existentialist analysis of
human existence we have an adequate means for interpreting
the New Testament kerygma so that contemporary man can
understand. He will understand it in terms of the meaning of
his existence which, in this view, is a unity with that view of
New Testament man.

The terminology of existentialist thought has been discussed
elsewhere and will not be repeated here. However, one needs
to remember that Heidegger has only systematized and given
philosophical explanation to an understanding of human existence which is usually associated with the name of Sören Kierkegaard. Kierkegaard was definitely and admittedly indebted
to the New Testament for his understanding of such existence.
Bultmann approaches his theological interpretation from the
standpoint that the message is about man's understanding of
his own existence. God is not known objectively like some
thing. God is known only in personal existence. A certain
subjective element is always present in this type of thinking.
Bultmann readily admits this and applies it to his own understanding of history itself. History is not a matter of objective

happenedness, but rather it is *Geschichte*, in which events have meaning that continues to confront us with decision in the area of personal existence.

The New Testament understands life apart from faith as a life under the power of cosmic forces. The source of this bondage is not in the material nature of man but in his sinfulness. Such life is inauthentic. When man lives in search of security, he is weighed down by anxiety and falls under the domination of "powers." His drive for physical and visible security causes him to collide with other men, and together they create an environment of sinfulness. He grasps for life and possessions, all the while knowing secretly that they are slipping away from him.

In the New Testament, authentic life is not based upon such tangible realities. Rather, authentic existence is "life after the Spirit," or "life in faith." But only the grace of God makes it possible. God's grace liberates man from his sinful past and grants him faith's possibility, openness to the future.[13] Such openness is a kind of detachment from the world, yet is quite different from asceticism. Bultmann likes to call it eschatological existence. Eschatology usually designates "last things," but Bultmann uses the term to describe a type of existence in the present. Faith brings the "end" of faith into the present, so that Paul could describe it as bringing about a new creature in the place of the old (2 Cor. 5:17).

John's Gospel gives such an interpretation of the eschatological hope. Faith expresses the idea that man is on the way toward the goal, but the goal is real in his life already. This new life is the authentic life, and it is known by faith in Jesus Christ.

OBJECTIONS TO DEMYTHOLOGIZING AND BULTMANN'S RESPONSES

A number of objections could naturally be raised by Bultmann's critics, but most of these were anticipated by him. One such objection could be phrased in the question, "Can one

come to Christian understanding of existence without having
faith in Christ?" Bultmann's answer to this is found in the
original essay.[14] The existentialist understanding of existence
is a philosophical view through which the Christian understanding can be clarified and the New Testament interpreted.
New Testament faith is always in Jesus Christ and such faith
only became possible at this definite point in history as a result
of the event of Jesus Christ. In spite of the logic of the question and the desirability of an affirmative answer, Bultmann's
appreciation of history (*Geschichte*) leads him to acknowledge that such faith has not in fact happened apart from the
New Testament event of Christ.[15] The New Testament portrays
a view of sin which incapacitates man. Knowing what he
"ought" to be is quite different from being it. Man is a sinner
who can be delivered only by the act of God. The "crucial
difference" between the New Testament and existentialism is
that the New Testament "speaks and faith knows of an act of
God through which man becomes capable of self-commitment,
capable of faith and love, of authentic life."[16] Existentialism
tells him what it is but is unable to deliver him from the
despair which results when he is unable to achieve it.

Would not the event of Jesus Christ, and God's act in him,
be mythical, and therefore a legitimate subject for demythologizing? Bultmann's reply is a willingness to demythologize
the event of Jesus Christ, but to insist that it is still an "act of
God." He stresses that the New Testament evidence about
Jesus is contradictory in such instances as one view about
Jesus' human life in Nazareth and the other idea of his pre-
existence. To him, this is a combination of myth and history.
He thinks it impossible to reconcile Paul's doctrine of pre-
existence and Matthew's "legend" of the virgin birth. So, he
sees these as attempts to emphasize the meaning of Jesus for
faith and, for that reason, they do not have to be taken objectively. The mythological language forbids one to understand
Jesus in simple historical terms, but stresses that his origin
transcends "both history and nature."[17]

What does demythologizing do to the cross? While he thinks that much of the language in the New Testament about the cross is mythological, the cross itself is historical and indispensable for faith. He rejects all interpretations in which the cross is seen as a sacrifice to change God (or man in some objective, external way), but insists that the cross means that by faith we may existentially undergo crucifixion with Christ (Rom. 6:6). The cross, though it happened historically long ago, is not an event of long ago, but rather is an ever-present event. In it, by faith, our sins, lusts, etc., are crucified, and we become new creatures. It is a permanent fact of meaningful history, not a past event of mythological history.

Is the resurrection mythical? The resurrection and the cross are inseparable in the New Testament. Bultmann thinks it is inconceivable to speak of the resurrection as a "historical" event (resuscitation of a corpse), which would somehow validate the power and meaning of the cross. Even though the New Testament presents it so, verified by the physical senses, Bultmann regards it as an affirmation of the article of faith on resurrection. It is more important than a single historical event proved by an empty tomb. It is an eschatological event in which man may participate by faith. Christians participate in the death and resurrection of Christ in everyday life. Faith in the resurrection is not assenting to a lesson of ancient history. There is no proof. Faith is not vindication by historical research. The risen Christ encounters us through preaching. Proof would make faith unnecessary. The proclamation of the resurrection is part of the eschatological event of redemption and not a result of it.[18]

In such a program of demythologizing, is any act of God possible? The question is serious and Bultmann so regarded it. His theology rests on the event of Christ within which God acted to redeem. The critics argued that one must either go on and demythologize the "act of God" or even the idea of "God," or admit the necessity of retaining mythology in order to retain the ideas of God and that God acts. Bultmann's re-

sponse is that his critics are opposing on the ground that they
understand God's act as "intervening" between the natural or
historical events in the sense of breaking the cause-effect
chain.[19] Rather, he understands the act of God as happening
"within" these events. This action is not subject to historical
observation (it is hidden), but is known only to the eye of
faith. Bultmann is quick to acknowledge that some would
regard his view as "pantheistic piety," with God being immanent in all affairs,[20] but on the ground of faith he denies the
charge. For instance, the incident of the healing of a sick
child can be seen completely in natural terms of cause and
effect, but one can give thanks to God. There is a paradox of
faith in which one can understand an event as an act of God
and at the same time see a completely intelligible explanation
in natural or historical terms.

Would not Bultmann's program of demythologizing replace
the mythological world view with a modern scientific world
view which could then become the same hindrance to understanding the message? The answer is yes. But, Bultmann replies[21] that demythologizing does not reject the Scripture of
the Christian message but only the world view of the past.
God's Word in the Christian proclamation is personal; it calls
men to personal decision. The present world view will change,
but the program of demythologizing would itself prevent the
equation of the message with the prevalent world view. This
is Bultmann's point. Modern man cannot believe in evil
spirits, demons, a personal Satan, and a three-story universe
with heaven above, hell below, etc. Transcendence in the New
Testament portrays God "up there," but Bultmann would
insist that in demythologizing God's transcendence is not only
retained but is also clarified as God standing before us and
liberating us for a radical openness to the future.[22]

Would not demythologizing transform faith into a philosophy, or at least subordinate it to existentialist philosophy?
Bultmann argues that every interpreter approaches the text
with certain presuppositions and questions. Happily, he ac-

knowledges that Heidegger's existentialist analysis provided
an orderly approach for him. It enables him to ask the right
questions. However, he quickly denies to philosophy the power
to produce faith and consistently argues for the uniqueness
of Christian faith in Christ, and the power of the Holy Spirit.
Existentialist philosophy is not ultimate. In faith, man knows
God.

Would not demythologizing reduce God to a merely subjective human experience? If God is known only in human
existence, would not the objective existence of God be in question? To be sure, Bultmann says "to speak of God is to speak
of myself . . . ," but "it by no means follows that God is not
outside the believer." [23] Since we know God only in personal
response, subject to subject, to his address to us, we can never
speak of God objectively but only in terms of what he does to
and with us.[24]

Does not demythologizing destroy the once-for-allness of
the event of Christ? Christians believe that Christ died once
for all, for the whole world (Rom. 6:10). Bultmann replies
that the unique event is Jesus Christ, but the point is not the
historical happenedness in an event which was "once" and is
therefore valid "for all." The point is that that event is eschatological. That God was in Christ is not a fact subject to historical proof. It is the kind of event which happens in any age
when the Word is preached. He comes here and now in the
gospel, and this is the eschatological once-for-all element.[25]
The uniqueness is not that God entered the evil world at one
particular historical age, but that he enters *our* evil age.[26]

In summary, one may do well to consider what is involved
in Bultmann's task of interpretation. Carl Michalson [27] has
seen three things at stake in this process. (1) The church's
message itself is at stake. Bultmann's problem was that of
trying to show modern man that the message of God in the
New Testament is authentic and that one does not have to sub-
scribe to a pre-Copernican view of the world before understanding and grasping faith. If modern man ties his faith to

such an outmoded view of the world, he will guarantee that
faith will go out of existence.

(2) The idea of justification by faith alone is at stake. Myth
looks upon the realities of faith as if they were provable
(1 John 1:1). Bultmann rejects every such security and proof,
and on New Testament grounds. For instance, "doubting
Thomas" was reprimanded with the reminder that it would
have been better had he not demanded "proof" (John 20:29).
Myths objectify God and his acts so that faith is not possible
or necessary.

(3) The uniqueness of Christ is at stake. Bultmann thinks
that the New Testament mythology intended to show the
uniqueness of Christ, but had the opposite effect. Christ is
unique, but the uniqueness is that "when he speaks, God's word
is heard by men as the meaning of their existence." [28]

VI. Existential Speaking "of" God

Whether it be conscious or unconscious, man's life is impelled by "the question of God." [1] Yet, Bultmann is very reluctant to talk directly about God. He makes a sharp distinction between God and a "concept of God." [2] To frame a concept of God is to objectify God and, hence, to make an idol. This is speaking "about" God as if he were an object of knowledge. But, God is really known only by the individual in faith's response to God's Word, and one can only speak "of" God in the personal sense of confession. Nevertheless, it is still necessary to speak "about" God, in spite of the danger of objectifying God, since the subject of theology is God. [3]

Bultmann's theological thought is grounded in biblical faith and is expressed primarily in biblical terminology. He also shows a preference for those emphases which are distinctive among the dialectical theologians. He speaks of God as Creator, wholly other, transcendent, the God who acts, the God of revelation, and the hidden God.

SPEAKING "ABOUT" GOD

In his 1934 sermon entitled "Faith in God the Creator," [4] based on 1 Cor. 8:4–6, which deals with eating food offered to idols, Bultmann pointed out that for Christians there is "one God, the Father, from whom are all things and for whom

we exist, ánd one Lord, Jesus Christ, through whom are all
things and through whom we exist." This means that God
stands above the powers of nature, history, nation, and all of
life, and claims us for himself.[5] God created the world out of
nothing, so all created things have their existence only from
him. Without God's sustaining power, the creatures would
fall into nothingness. If our existence is not in God, it is nothing at all.

To speak of God as Creator is not to hold a world view, but
to be aware that we are creatures, dependent upon God, having no permanence of our own. It means to know of the nothingness of the world and ourselves apart from God the
Creator.[6] Christians believe that God the Creator acted in the
cross of Christ to give them existence. The cross is God's judgment on man and the crucifixion of his pride. To believe is to
be crucified with Christ. To sin is to forget that one is a creature and to assume that one has divine and creative power
within himself. Man is always tempted by the powers of the
world to forget that he is a creature and thereby to surrender
his freedom.

Bultmann's idea of transcendence is in evidence in his view
of God as Creator, but also in other areas. Along with other
dialectical theologians he speaks of God as wholly other, and
alludes to the sharp line of demarcation between God and
man reminiscent of Martin Luther. His deep reverence for the
transcendent God shows in the way he speaks of the mystery,
infiniteness, and hiddenness of God.[7] His view is especially
clear in his essay on liberal theology[8] in which he pointed out
not only that liberalism was concerned with man instead of
God, but also that liberalism's inordinate dependence on
history amounted to a historical guarantee for faith. In short,
this made God so immanent that a sort of "pantheism in history" resulted. Bultmann objected that "God is other than
the world, he is beyond the world."[9]

The transcendence of God in biblical thought is distinct
from that of Greek thought. The Greek conception of tran-

scendence was that of mind over the material and sensual world. It was timelessness over history. In biblical faith transcendence points to the absolute authority in which God is independent of all powers. He is God as Creator, who is Lord of history [10] and his basic nature is will.[11]

The only knowledge of God comes in his revelation. While Bultmann appreciates philosophy much more than Karl Barth does, he does not believe that man can "know" God apart from revelation. In the 1941 essay, "The Question of Natural Revelation," he summarized statements that could be said "about" God on the basis of philosophy, but went on to point out that while Christian belief would confirm such a "concept of God," philosophy is really talking "about" God but cannot know God. The Christian asserts that other statements about God are illusions and that God is known only in his revelation in Christ. In fact, even such talking about God's transcendence is sin.[12] This general knowledge is not revelation apart from Christ.[13]

The revelation of God has its chief event in Christ. The essay, "The Concept of Revelation in the New Testament" (1929), makes a distinction between revelation as a communication of knowledge by the Word, and revelation as "an occurrence that puts me in a new situation as a self." [14] Revelation is personal address consisting not in *what*, but *that* God comes in the event of Jesus Christ. "Thus revelation consists in nothing other than the fact of Jesus Christ." [15] It is not the communication of knowledge, but an occurrence which calls me to God and to authentic existence. So, we can say that Bultmann really believes that God has revealed himself in Jesus Christ but not to convey information. Therefore, we cannot say what God is like. We cannot portray him objectively. We can only respond by faith and thus know him existentially.

It sounds almost traditional for Bultmann to say that God *acts* to redeem man. But Bultmann rejects the idea of miraculous intervention. He remarks that the idea of miracle has become "untenable and it must be abandoned." [16] The only "wonder" is God's revelation of himself to the ungodly in the form of forgiveness, which is God's act.[17] Ian Henderson has suggested that Bultmann has left no room for God to act and yet insists that he "acts."[18] Bultmann's explanation entitled "The Meaning of God as Acting"[19] maintains that it would be mythological language to say that God broke in from the outside and interrupted the cause-effect relationship of nature and history so as to perform a miracle. But he maintains that he speaks "analogically" and not "mythologically." God acts *in* events which may have a causal explanation. We speak of God as acting only when speaking of our own existence. God's action is hidden except to the eyes of faith. Furthermore, the encounter of God cannot be known in some general or timeless way. It is known only in a "specific event here and now."[20]

Consequently, there is no summary of what Bultmann says "about" God. He did discuss Jesus' idea of God, which was essentially Jewish but with one exception. In the Jewish idea, God was historicized and bound to the nation, whereas Jesus understood God to be interested primarily in individuals.[21] Of course, God is—he exists—but I cannot frame a verbal portrait of him without making an idol. It is immaterial whether one uses philosophical language or biblical language in making such an idol. However, I can respond to God's Word to me in the kerygma and know him.

SPEAKING "OF" GOD

Several distinctive convictions "of" God appear in the writings of Bultmann. These can be detected as early as 1925 in the essay "What Does It Mean to Speak of God."[22] As late as 1963, he wrote an essay in response to Bishop Robinson's *Honest To God* and the ensuing discussion. In this essay, "The Idea of God and Modern Man,"[23] he makes some clarifications but no basic changes.

God is not an object and, consequently, cannot be known or discussed as if he were a given entity. Bultmann rejects the subject-object scheme in theology so characteristic of Western thought, since it looks upon the subject God as if it were an object of investigation. It is talk "about" God and takes the viewpoint outside of God. God does not permit man to speak of him in general propositional statements. Bultmann clarifies with the analogy of love. It makes no sense to talk "about" love, because in the moment one speaks "about" love, he has taken a theoretical position outside of love and has therefore abandoned love itself. Love is known only in life as one actually loves another or is loved. To make theoretical statements "about" God is to take a position outside of God and also to put oneself outside his own true reality. So, such talk is not only erroneous but, since it is "outside" God, it is also atheistic and sinful.[24]

The foregoing argument is valid since theoretical talk about God assumes a position of neutrality. To assume such a position of neutrality with reference to God is to abandon the idea of God. Bultmann employs an illustration from Luther's interpretation of Genesis in which the sin of Adam is discussed. Adam's sin was not eating forbidden fruit, but it was questioning God by setting himself apart and arguing "about" what God had said. All such talk "about" God, even if it employs biblical language and arises from a sincere knowledge of God, falls into the category of sin precisely because in that moment one is speaking objectively. One rather must speak "of" God who determines his existence and claims him.[25]

Therefore, if one speaks of God, he must simultaneously "speak of himself."[26] It is also possible to stand outside of, and objectify, our own existence in such a way as to destroy it. Man can speak "of" God only in terms of his own existence, and this means his personal, individual, involved, and deciding existence. God is real only to the man whose existence is being determined by God, who is responding in obedience to God's claim. To take an outside or neutral position and talk about this claim or the God who made it would be a repudiation of God's claim.[27] So, when a Christian speaks of God's

transcendence he means that God is not at man's disposal. To
speak of God as wholly other is to speak against the background of man's existence. One is saying that his own existence is godless or sinful. Sinful man tries to free himself by
fleeing from God, who alone determines man's existence.
When man sees himself as a sinner, it makes sense to speak
of God as wholly other.

The Christian idea of revelation further illustrates that
speaking of God is also speaking of oneself. Revelation is
never the disclosure of information "about" God, but rather
the personal disclosure "of" God in encounter with man.
Man hears God's Word in his own personal existence. It is
intensely personal and subjective, so we cannot talk about
God without talking in these personal terms. (However, talking about one's own existence is not necessarily talking of
God.) In the 1963 essay, Bultmann restated that revelation in
Christian faith is about an act of God not visible to the objectifying thought of reason. It is an event which does not com-
municate doctrines, but gives man power to be authentic and
to know that he is sustained by God.[28] With appreciation, he
quoted Dietrich Bonhoeffer's *Letters and Papers from Prison*
and spoke of God's transcendence as being found "not above
or beyond" the world, but rather in the "midst of this world."

Does not the implied subjectivism mean that it is impossible, therefore, to speak either about God or about human
existence? Bultmann thinks the problem is the deeply en-
trenched subject-object relationship which has prevailed since
the time of Descartes. This type of thinking, influenced by
Greek science but relatively modern, isolates subject from
object. Man sees himself as the subject and all other things,
even persons, as objects. He makes an object of anything or
person he knows. Bultmann thinks this is the error. In biblical
thought, the world and God are not objectified. The task of
theology is to overcome this subject-object scheme of thought
by seeing the subject-subject, personal, existential nature of
man.

World views are always ideologies constructed by man to relieve him of the anxieties and responsibilities in his existence. These views are deceptive in that they impose a comfortable unity on a world filled with threats, responsibilities, etc. A world view may even include God, but in a misleading way. Human existence is filled with care and responsibility. Man is always in danger. But, his subjective type of existence does not allow him to evade responsibility for existence by creating a false objective world which he can manage. And, he certainly must not change God into an objective portrait (idol) which he can keep at his disposal.

It may appear that man's logical course of action is to say nothing at all about God—to remain silent. Bultmann concurs with this decision except in one instance—when man *must* speak of God. The necessity is not derived from some external authority. It is not derived from pious obligation or psychological necessity. When God speaks to us within our own existential being and we respond in free decision by faith, we must speak of God.

Man can speak "of" God, but only when he speaks in faith. This is really the meaning of faith. Nothing else is. We know our own existence only in faith, and we know God only in faith. We speak "of" God in the context of his grace and the forgiveness of sins. God is transcendent and man is sinful. Man cannot know "about" God, and yet, God speaks to sinful man and gives him new life. Then, man can speak "of" God in the personal terms of obedience and confession. But, he can never prove God. He can only respond in faith and speak "of" him. Bultmann reiterates the warning that it is dangerous, even though necessary, to talk "about" God. He concluded his early essay on the subject with these words:

> Even this lecture is a speaking about God and as such, if God is, it is sin, and if God is not, it is meaningless. Whether it has meaning and whether it is justified—none of us can judge.[29]

VII. Ground of Faith – The Christ Event

As a Christian theologian, Bultmann's primary concern has been to understand the event of Christ and to interpret the meaning of that event to others. While his appraisers rate his work all the way from rank heresy to the greatest New Testament scholarship of the century, he considers his radical attempt to demythologize the New Testament a perfect parallel to the efforts of Paul and Luther to stress the doctrine of justification by faith alone apart from the works of Law.[1]

Along with other Christian theologians, Bultmann maintains that Christian faith is grounded in the event of Jesus Christ. Unlike most other theologians, he has little interest in the historical Jesus. However, he leaves no doubt but that he regards Christian faith as committed to the idea that the decisive *act of God,* and the central idea of the New Testament, is the redemptive act in the person of Jesus Christ.[2] Although some readers may stumble at his lack of interest in Jesus, there is some reassurance in his emphasis that faith is not definable in the abstract, but is always "faith *in* Christ." To Bultmann, Christ is not the kind of event to be defined as *Historie* but as *Geschichte,* an event which continues to impinge upon the life of man. Jesus Christ is the singular historic event which brings man into God's presence.

GOD'S SAVING ACT

We have already noted that Bultmann is most vulnerable at the point of maintaining that God acted in Christ to redeem man while at the same time insisting that in demythologizing one must abandon the notion that God intervenes or interrupts the normal course of history or nature. Does not this dilemma reduce the whole concept of Christian revelation and redemption to a subjective experience? Bultmann insists that the answer is "No!" The dilemma appears impossible because one is talking theoretically "about" God as if he were outside, and not "of" God in terms of human existence.

The event of Christ must be regarded as a real and objective act of history. It is not pictorial or symbolical. The events happened, but the bare events did not disclose the act of God. For instance, Pilate and Caiaphas observed the historical Jesus, but this was no act of God to them. Bultmann asserts that when I speak of an act of God I am always speaking of my own existence, since I know God only in the personal existence of faith-commitment. Man does not live life generally and does not know existence in general, but in a specific, individual, here-and-now sense. Consequently, if I hear the Word of God in the proclamation calling me to faith, I know the act of God. But I know this act of God only *in* faith.[3] Again, Bultmann insists *that* God acted in Christ. "At the very point where man can do nothing, God steps in and acts— indeed he has acted already—on man's behalf."[4] But this event cannot be known as other historical acts are known, nor can it be described as to its *what* and *how*.

The act of God in Christ is known existentially, just as man can only talk of God in terms of human existence. For instance, forgiveness of sins is an event which may rightly be called an act of God. Although Bultmann clearly rejects the traditional view of miracle as God's breaking into history or nature and interrupting its cause-and-effect sequence, he regards the forgiveness of sins as a "wonder" and an act of God.[5] He views traditional language about miracle as mythological and therefore in need of existential interpretation. Existential understanding employs analogical thinking—the analogy between the activity of God and man, and the analogy between God and man—rather than mythological.[6]

Therefore, while natural happenings are discernible to natural observation, the acts of God are discernible to the eyes of faith only. God's acts are hidden within normal historical events and are revealed to men in faith.[7]

God's saving act in the historical Jesus is a historic event. Men in faith came to know God. When they proclaim that event, others come to faith. So, proclamation of the event is a continuation of the event and, consequently, a part of the event.

CROSS AND RESURRECTION

The specific saving act of God is the cross and resurrection.[8] Bultmann maintains that the cross and resurrection are central and inseparable, both in his early essays [9] and in his later works.[10] Christ's death and resurrection constitute the "salvation-occurrence." [11] In Paul's theology, which Bultmann appreciates, the very act of God's saving grace was that he "gave Christ up to die on the cross." [12] Paul was not concerned with the details of Jesus' life, but considered Christ's death and resurrection the act of God's prevenient grace. It is equally significant that the cross and resurrection are looked upon as a single event (Rom. 10:9).

Bultmann regards the cross as a purely historical event, but he sees the resurrection as an assertion of faith. The fact that the cross is historical introduces an element of ambiguity not present in the resurrection. It tempts men to see the resurrection as the validation of the saving power of the cross and to try to go "behind" the proclamation of the cross and the resurrection to find some provable fact. Bultmann argues that to Paul, as well as to him, the important factor is *that* the cross and resurrection are the saving event. This leads to the proclamation, which is all-important to Bultmann. It is the proclamation of the cross and resurrection that becomes the saving act of God.[13]

Bultmann has very little regard for the traditional theories (attempts to explain how Christ's cross accomplished atonement) of the work of Christ. He thinks that Paul employed both the expiatory, sacrificial language of Judaism and the redeemer myth of Gnostic thought, but was actually trying to show what happened to man existentially when he believes in Christ's cross and resurrection.

Many interpretations of faith in Christ presuppose that prior to the decision of trust, one has learned the basic information about Christ and has come to believe that it is true. Bultmann denies this twofold coming to faith. Rather, he sees a single decisive event in Paul's theology. The gospel confronts man with a single demand for decision. This is best seen in Paul's teaching on justification by faith. Prior to his faith in Christ, Paul sought justification by his own works within the Law and was guilty of boasting of his own righteousness. The proclamation of the cross and resurrection came as a shattering blow which demanded that he abandon his own boasting and trust in Christ's cross and resurrection. This call happens nowhere else but in the proclamation of Christ.[14] Therefore the cross and resurrection in the proclamation constitute a single event which is both historical and historic.

The cross and resurrection came to Paul as a sheer act of God's grace demanding of him a completely new self-understanding. The Law had not been burdensome to Paul. He had loved it, thought it was good (Rom. 7:12), and later saw Christian faith as the fulfillment of it (Rom. 13:8–10). But Paul did not know that victory by obeying the Law would have been a victory of the flesh,[15] and that it would burden him with self-glorying. The gospel of the cross and resurrection required a renunciation of all self-glorying and a surrender to the grace of God. This is the radical new self-understanding Paul knew in faith. The cross and resurrection wiped out Paul's ground of boasting by disqualifying Judaism and the Law.

Although Bultmann considers cross and resurrection as a single event, an event of redemption, it needs to be remem-

bered that he does not regard the resurrection as historical.
Of course, the cross is historical in the sense that anyone
could have seen the crucifixion. He denies the physical resurrection (resuscitation of a corpse) as "utterly inconceivable!" [16] Even though the New Testament writers see the
resurrection as proof of the power of the cross, Bultmann
disregards even Paul's citation of the resurrection appear-
ances as proofs or a guarantee for faith.[17] He regards the
cross as historical in the sense that it happened as any other
event in ancient history. However, that the cross was an act of
God, or related to man's salvation, is purely an assertion of
faith. It is historic but not historical.

Cross and resurrection together form the historic and eschatological event of man's salvation. In the proclamation, the
cross and resurrection are not past but contemporary. The
event is primarily eschatological; it brings a new age. Cross
and resurrection ultimately mean the same thing—God's salvation.

PROCLAMATION OF THE KERYGMA AS SAVING ACT

In response to the question as to how we come to believe that
the cross and resurrection form the unique eschatological
belief, Bultmann responds that Christ meets us in the preaching of the cross and resurrection. "Faith comes by hearing
. . . the preaching of Christ" (Rom. 10:17). This can only
mean that the proclamation is a part of, or continuation of,
the saving act of God. Bultmann maintains that this proclamation is not the mere repetition of something which happened previously, but is a part of the saving event, since the
"ground of faith is solely Word of proclamation." [18] The
preaching is not preliminary or preparatory instruction to be
later followed up by or utilized in the demand to decide for
Christ. The gospel is the demand for faith which brings one
to the new self-understanding when he acknowledges Christ

of the kerygma as Lord. Therefore, salvation "happens" only in the proclaiming and hearing of the proclamation of Christ.

Faith can have no other ground if it is to remain faith. It cannot be legitimated by known or yet-to-be-known facts about Jesus. Such a procedure would make faith dependent upon historical research. Faith does not consist of coming to the intellectual conclusion that Jesus was crucified outside the north wall of Jerusalem in the long ago. Rather, faith consists of that trustful response of man to the preached cross in which he knows the power of salvation, freedom from sin and guilt, and a new relationship to God. Rejecting ancient and modern proofs for a literal resurrection of Christ, Bultmann affirms that the "risen Christ is present in the proclaiming word." [19] Christ is not like some ancient hero who may inspire men. He is the eschatological saving event who demands that the sinner decide for faith.

CHRIST AS THE WORD OF GOD

The dialectical theologians have a special love for the "Word" of God, and Bultmann is no exception. His assertions about the Christ event and the proclamation lead to the affirmation that "Christ is himself the Word." [20] In the essay, "The Concept of the Word of God in the New Testament," [21] he points out that in the Old Testament, God's Word was both his actions and his deeds and that it had its own power. God spoke it as an event and it was understood as God's address or summons to man. [22] Therefore, God's Word, as an address to man, is really God himself present with man. Consequently, "hearing" God is really an encounter with him. Apparently, Jesus followed this Old Testament understanding of the Word and was a proclaimer of the Word which confronted hearers with a demand to decide.

The Old Testament idea of God's Word as creative, powerful, and judging is also present in the New Testament, but the New Testament also knows the Word as the Christian proclamation.[23] This word appears to be thought of as human speech to men, but it also is the Word of God. It, too, is always a summons to decision, demanding that man acknowledge God, and is understood only when it is "heard." Therefore, it is a call for faith, but also an event that takes place in man's existential self-understanding. The Word of God is not a system of ideas, but a Word addressed to man. The Word is Christ himself (John 1:14).

The preaching of the Word is a "continuation of the Christ event."[24] Therefore, it follows that, if Christ is present in the preaching of the Word, and if men know the power of the cross only through this preaching, Bultmann has good reason for not trying to go behind the proclamation as if to verify it. His concern is that it really is the Word of God and is still being heard. The Word is the eschatological, ever-present event of Christ in preaching.

In the Word, God's saving act is ever-present. When the messengers proclaim it (Rom. 10:13–17), God personally addresses sinful men, calling them into radical questioning, a new self-understanding and authentic existence—faith.[25]

So, preaching is God's saving act, not communicating information about past events which may, or may not, be established apart from faith. It is God's eschatological event of salvation.[26] If this is true, then preaching today is no different from the preaching on the first Easter Sunday.

THE CHRIST EVENT AS REVELATION

The heart of Bultmann's *Theology of the New Testament* is a treatment of the respective theologies of John and Paul. He regards them as being in agreement on the major themes,[27] such as the saving act of God in Christ. However, Paul stressed the cross and resurrection as central, in contrast to John who stressed the whole idea of the incarnation. Walter Schmithals thinks Bultmann's bold contrast between the two at this point leads to the statement that "Good Friday and Easter are the Pauline feasts, Christmas and Epiphany the Johannine ones." [28]

To John, the event of the incarnation is God's revelation.[29] John interpreted the Son of God as God's messenger of light sent into a world of darkness (John 1:5; 3:19). God's love sent the Son so that men may come to *know* God and believe. The coming of Jesus was the great eschatological event [30] which was also his judgment on the world. God's Son came into the world as a human being, not communicating something about God, but calling men *to* God. Those who had seen the Son had seen the Father (John 14:9), for the Father and the Son are one (John 10:30). The whole point is not some view of atonement, nor even cross and resurrection as for Paul, but that all of the salvation event has been compressed into a single event—"the Revelation of God's 'reality' " [31]— in the earthly life of Jesus as known in man's faith.

The revelation is the same as the Word of God, since the works and words of Jesus are identical (John 6:68; 5:24; 8:51; 15:3; 17:17). Since Jesus is the way, the truth, and the life (John 14:6), he and his message are identical and he is rightly called the Word (John 1:1, 14). Then, what is the content of revelation?

Revelation is God's self-disclosure. Bultmann, in true dialectical fashion, never tires of pointing out that revelation does not consist of propositional truth about God, but is God's disclosure of himself.[32] Bultmann would object to my term "content" of revelation because of its objectifying implication. Revelation is God in Christ putting man in a new situation.[33]

Since revelation is the appearance of God in Christ, it answers no questions for the curious bystander. Instead, it calls its hearers into a radical questioning about existence. Christ did not come to relieve the kind of ignorance man could alleviate by study. Rather he came that men might know God who can forgive sinners. Revelation is personal address.[34] The emphasis in the New Testament is *that* God has disclosed himself rather than *what* has been disclosed. It happened in Jesus Christ, so Bultmann can say, "Thus revelation consists in nothing other than the fact of Jesus Christ." [35]

God's revelation in Christ confronts man with a choice. God's revelation is not the disclosure of interesting information about God, but rather the demand that man abandon the world and his own fallenness and live by faith in the Word which is Jesus Christ.[36] This decision involves the new self-understanding man has in Christ.

It is permissible to speak of natural revelation, or of revelation in history, but this revelation only tells us that we do not possess it.[37] Such revelation only refers us to the grace of God known only in Christ. Then, it is not really revelation until it is in Christ. Revelation is not really natural, or general, but only specific and individual.

Revelation is the occurrence to the individual man when the Word is proclaimed to him. He chooses faith, without any validation by miracle either in history or in nature. But in his own existence he knows God through Christ.

VIII. Existence Prior to Faith—Inauthentic Existence

Heidegger does not talk of sin and faith or God as does Bultmann. Rather, he speaks of human existence as being either inauthentic or authentic. These two words are the secular equivalents of the biblical terms "sin" and "faith." Bultmann speaks reluctantly "about" God, but his theology rests firmly upon the belief that God is, and that man's only authentic life is by faith in God who confronts him in this world demanding obedience. Since God is the ultimate norm, then sin is understood primarily as lack of faith or as unbelief.

SIN AS UNBELIEF

One does not understand sin except in the light of the revelation of faith.[1] It is as if sin slumbers in man until God's commandment comes to him, thus awakening it (Rom. 7:9).[2] Man knows that he is a sinner only in the light of standing before God in the knowledge of grace. So, the definition of sin in retrospect emphasizes that sin, when finally recognized for what it is, is really unbelief. Bultmann cites John 15:22, "If I had not come and spoken to them, they would not have sin; but now they have no excuse for their sin." Revelation not only brings the opportunity for faith but also the awareness of sin. Bultmann concludes, "The real sin is unbelief."[3]

Paul portrays the life of unbelief as life "according to the flesh" (Rom. 8:4) in contrast to the life of faith which is life "according to the Spirit." When Paul described human existence in terms of the body (*soma*), he was not designating the physical aspect as opposed to the spiritual, but man's whole person.[4] In the *soma*-concept, man is such that he has a relationship with himself which can either be proper or counterfeit. Since he is able to distinguish between himself (self from himself), he is aware of outside powers which bid for control of his life. One of these powers is "flesh" (*sarx*). *Sarx* is not literal flesh, even though in some cases it is merely carnality. Distinctively, "flesh" in Paul's usage designates man's bodily existence given over to sin. Just as life in faith is "according to the Spirit," so life "according to the flesh" is life in unbelief. Man stands before God and must decide. The proper response is faith. Other responses amount to unbelief.[5]

Human existence characterized by self-glorying is basically life prior to, or without, faith. Pride is close to the very essence of sin. Bultmann never, wearies of contrasting the righteousness which is by radical faith, and that which man attempts to achieve for himself. Paul is his New Testament source. In the 1940 essay, "Christ the End of the Law,"[6] he developed this theme fully. All attempts of man to secure his own salvation, whether by guarantees from history, by miracles in nature, or by theology, or even by God, portray man's basic self-glorying. Man must have some ground for pride or boasting. Paul knew this essential characteristic of fallenness all too well (Rom. 3:27; 1 Cor. 9:15, 16). Faith in Christ calls for a renunciation of all such self-glorying and a complete abandonment to God.

Another illustration of sin as unbelief comes as the result of man's self-glorying. Man constructs a religion of works, in which he tries to hide his unbelief. Paul's discussion of the Law is the classic example. The Law, though good in itself, was changed into a means of acquiring credit with God so as to make faith unnecessary. All attempts of man to provide a guarantee or substitute for faith amount to unbelief, and hence, existence without God. Bultmann defined man's "*real sin*" as not consisting of sins, but rather as the "*basic attitude of man*" known in trying to "*establish his own righteousness.*"[7] The Pharisee and the publican illustrate clearly the contrast intended.[8]

Life in unbelief involves a certain understanding of self which has been implied in the self-glorying tendency of man. Bultmann stresses the radical change made by faith in this self-understanding. In unbelief, man understands himself in terms of self. When faith comes, man sees himself in relationship to God.

When man does not believe in God, he clings to self and has an attachment to the world which is inauthentic. He seeks to validate himself in the world and thus becomes a part of it, "of-the-world." When faith comes, man lets go of the world and learns a certain detachment from the world, which is not any kind of asceticism but an abandonment of false security.[9]

Bultmann thinks that the self-centeredness which marks the life of unbelief is basically what the church has tried to say in its doctrine of original sin.[10] It would be difficult to find more significant statements of sin as unbelief than that man wills "to be himself by himself and for himself,"[11] and that sinful man, though created for God, tries to seclude himself from other men and God and to live in his own self-centeredness.[12]

In conclusion, sin is the misunderstanding of oneself so that man forgets that he is a creature of God and then tries to put himself in God's place. Man's "primal sin" is understanding himself in purely selfish terms and without reference to God. It is putting confidence in the flesh.[13]

SIN AS SURRENDER TO THE WORLD

All human existence involves a relationship to the world. Heidegger's term for human existence (*Dasein*) means "being-in-the-world." But Heidegger stressed the necessity for man, if he is to have authentic existence, to distinguish between himself and the world. When man loses the distinction and chooses to live out of the world, on the resources of the world, he loses his authentic existence. He becomes merely a part of the world, a part of the "they." He becomes "of-the-world" as well as "in-the-world." Bultmann has noted that the New Testament also sees the world as the area of life which man chooses when he rejects God.

Generally speaking, Paul designates the created world as "creation" since the term implies the Creator (Rom. 1:20, 25; 8:19, 20, 21, 23, 39). Man is God's creature, but partakes of a nature which places him higher than the rest of creation and nearer to God (1 Cor. 11:3, 7). To Paul, creation can be the earth which God has placed at man's disposal, or it can be the arena of demonic activity.[14] So, man chooses either to acknowledge God or to seek his life from the created world. If man could accomplish this living from the world without God he would have eliminated risk and uncertainty, since the world would be at his disposal. Paul's understanding of sin includes the idea that man tries to live without God. He tries to get life by his own power, and will not take it as a gift from its Creator.[15] This is life "according to the flesh."

Life according to the flesh (2 Cor. 10:2) is translated "worldly" (*kata sarka*) in the Revised Standard Version. This term has meaning for Paul. This sinful life is that surrendered to worldly pleasures, desires, frivolity, passion, or even to feverish religious activity. It is turning from God to the creation.[16] Man's natural care is thereby changed from concern to the attempt to secure oneself against the future by resorting to the resources of the world (1 Cor. 7:32–35; Phil. 4:6).[17]

John's understanding of the world is essentially the same as that of Paul.[18] It deals primarily with the world of men. Bultmann's subtitle, "The Perversion of the Creation into 'the World,'" is indicative of his interpretation of John's view of sin. It is fallenness into darkness and bondage to sinister powers. It is the attempt to live from the security of the world and without God. In a sermon on John 16:5–15, preached in Marburg on May 15, 1938, Bultmann explained that John did not intend "world" to mean nature, the area of our possibilities, nor even the creation of God. "World" is used in the specific sense as that sphere under the control of the prince of this world. He stressed that a man can surrender to this world in his very attempt to master it. It then holds sway over him. Paul also recognized and refused to be enslaved by these powers (1 Cor. 6:12). When human existence turns from God to this world, the world claims totalitarian power and becomes an all-sufficient god.[19] So, sin is slavery.

SIN AS SLAVERY

Since freedom is so important in the authentic existence of faith, there is no term any more suggestive of sin's disaster than the term "slavery." When man clings to his world and seeks his security in his own fallenness, having turned away from God who is his only hope, he is actually "sold under sin" (Rom. 7:14). The bondage becomes total. Man becomes the obedient slave of the cruel master (Rom. 6:16) who directs man's energies away from his true intention.[20] The seriousness of this slavery is obvious in the contrast with Christ's liberation of men from bondage (Rom. 6:6).

Paul indicated the universal threat of slavery. Men can be in bondage to the elemental spirits of pagan belief (Gal. 4:8f.). Men can also be in bondage to religious law with its useless observances (Gal. 4:1–10).[21] When man's slavery becomes complete, he boasts of his freedom, having come to believe that he finally has God at his disposal.

John, also, portrays sin as bondage.[22] Freedom is related to truth (John 8:32) and faith in God. Slavery is related to falsehood and the devil (John 8:44). Slavery is the kind of existence characterized by "this" world which is under the sway of the devil (John 12:31; 14:40; 16:11). The Jews who opposed Jesus in John's discussion (John 8) had fallen into a

religiously guaranteed slavery of the world with a resultant
darkness and falsehood to which they had become blind.

SIN AS DEATH

Inasmuch as death is such a prominent theme in existentialist
thought, it is both surprising and disappointing that Bultmann
did not fully develop this concept theologically. However, he
does point out that in sin man's quest for life ends only in
death.[23] Death is the punishment for and consequence of sin.
Man deserves death (Rom. 1:32) since he has earned his
"wages" (Rom. 6:23). Sin leads inevitably to death (Rom.
6:16). Bultmann thinks that Paul has gone beyond the legal
idea of debt in his interpretation of sin as death to the idea
that sin produces death because of an inner necessity, just as
a specific plant bears certain fruit.[24] The contrast is clearly
between the life of faith, which is life "according to the
Spirit," and the life of sin, which is life "according to the
flesh" (Rom. 8:13).

Ironically, the perverted striving of man after life produces
only death. Paul's presentation of this theme is based on a
religious striving (Rom. 7:7–25) in which he had diligently
engaged.

Bultmann noted that Paul did not reconcile his two ideas
of sin and death, punishment and consequence. John Macquarrie has suggested that Paul's idea of consequence for sin
may be but a deeper understanding of the punishment idea.
As such, it is a clearer indication of the relationship between
sin and death. He reasons that since inauthentic existence is a
loss of being, and since death likewise is a loss of being,
existentially the sinner is already dead.[25] Such a view is consistent with Bultmann and his view that death is also an existential reality in the present. The idea is certainly present in
Paul (Rom. 7:9, 11) and in John (1 John 3:14).

Heidegger's view of inauthentic existence is that of man
failing to decide in confidence to be himself in a world of

care and risk. He falls into the world and becomes a part of it by surrendering his true distinct existence. Slavery and "living" death are the consequences.

Bultmann understands the New Testament to teach that sin is inauthentic existence. Man was made for God, but in sin he tries to live without faith. Man is "in-the-world" but must not be "of-the-world." Sin is surrender to the world. Man was made to be free, but in sin he becomes a slave. Man was created for life, existence in the Spirit, but in sin he is dead already.

IX.
Life in Faith–Authentic Existence

We saw in the previous chapter that man without faith lives an inauthentic existence. He has a self-centered understanding of himself, which is actually pride. He rejects God in his attempt to live in the world. Religiously, he tries to establish his own righteousness while he rejects the gift of righteousness freely offered him. He clings to the world until his attachment becomes permanent. Then instead of being man, he is a parasite "of-the-world."

Faith is exactly the opposite. When faith happens, man comes to a new understanding of himself and his world. He surrenders to God in an act of radical decision. This decision is itself radical obedience to God and results in a genuine freedom from sin, world, self, law, and death. Negatively, this act of faith is a renunciation of the former self-understanding, the world and man's own righteousness. Positively, it is a response to God's Word in the cross and resurrection which results in an openness to God's future as it appears in any given moment. Faith is an eschatological occurrence which makes the authentic life one of hope and joy.

Faith is the most significant theme of Bultmann, and his entire hermeneutical effort has been spent in trying to clarify its meaning. Faith is the only corrective for sinful man who is living without meaning and direction, depending on a world in which he finds no security, living for self instead of for

God. Without faith man is a slave. In faith man is true and free man.

But faith has been misunderstood. Faith is not an abstract term and cannot be defined except as specific faith in Christ. It is not a general or universal term, but can be known and defined only as a specific act by an individual responding to God. Faith is never a work which man accomplishes. If it were, he would be inclined to be proud of himself.[1] Faith is not a set of doctrines which one believes.[2] It is not an experience of the past about which one reflects, or a state of the soul. Faith is the personal commitment of an individual to God.

Bultmann has defined the structure of faith as (1) obedience, (2) confession, (3) hope, (4) fear, and (5) confidence.[3] Obedience is acceptance of Jesus as Lord with the resultant change in one's self-understanding. As such, it prevents man from seeing faith as a "work," since it is both surrender and renunciation. Confession is the same as believing (Rom. 10:9) and prevents one from thinking of faith in the abstract. To believe is to confess Christ.[4] Confession is man's response to God's Word addressed to him in the gospel (Rom. 10:17). It is turning to God.[5]

Faith is hope, in that true faith points toward the future. As such, it creates the eschatological present.[6] Paul often refers to the present-aspect of salvation (1 Cor. 1:18; 2 Cor. 2:15) but also refers to the future hope (Rom. 8:24f.). Such hope is involved in Bultmann's interpretation of authentic existence as openness to the future.

Fear, usually thought of as opposed to faith, is considered by Bultmann to be a constitutive element in faith. It guarantees that man will keep looking to God's grace rather than to the world. Paul referred to his own weakness and fear (1 Cor. 2:1–5) and warned against pride (Rom. 11:20–22). He even "feared" Satan who lies in wait for believers (1 Thess. 3:5; 1 Cor. 7:5). This does not mean that fear and faith exist in some uneasy balance. It means that the threat of the world

remains and man must depend on God since he has a healthy
fear of the powers of the world.

Faith is confident since faith is hope, and since fear does
not overcome the faith in God. Because faith is trust in God's
saving deed, it can be confident.[7]

FAITH AS A NEW SELF-UNDERSTANDING

If one can speak of God only in terms of human existence,
and if we therefore interpret all of Christian faith in terms of
man's own existence, it is not surprising to find Bultmann
speaking of man's new self-understanding in faith. For instance, Bultmann contended that Paul's entire religious teaching could be described as a "new self-understanding."[8]

If faith is a new self-understanding, then there must have
been a previous self-understanding. This is precisely what
Bultmann described in man "prior to faith." Man understands himself in terms of belonging to the world. Self is his
center. Even in religious faith, his works allow him to understand himself so as to deserve God's verdict of righteousness.
The previous understanding has a preparatory role to fill for
man who comes to faith.

Even in sin, man has a "pre-understanding" about revelation and God, which, even though inadequate and erroneous,
prepares him to hear God's Word. In all of his interpretation, Bultmann maintains that it would be impossible to
understand a text without a pre-understanding. I must have
some such pre-understanding of its meaning, or of my own
possibilities, so that the text can speak to me.[9] For instance,
one does not understand literature, art, friendship, love, or
life without some previous knowledge. Even in sin, man has
this pre-understanding of his own existence, which makes it
possible for him to put the question to which revelation pro-
vides the right answer. Existentialist philosophy is important
because it gives man the proper understanding of existence
so as to have this pre-understanding for faith.

The new self-understanding of faith is a radically personal transformation. The individual is changed from a self-centered, isolated slave to the world into a new person with a new understanding of God, world, and self. Faith changes "my" whole world, and I understand myself in a completely new way.[10]

Pride vanishes in the new self-understanding along with the coming of faith as a pure gift of God. In the blindness of sin Paul did not recognize his fallenness. Faith removed the blinds and he saw himself in a new way.[11] The destruction of pride is the birthplace of Paul's joyful statements about the righteousness of faith.[12]

The confession that "Jesus is Lord" reflects not only a new understanding of Jesus but also a new understanding of self. For instance, Paul told of the revelation of Christ to him (Gal. 1:12–16) not meaning that God communicated certain factual knowledge which could have been obtained from other sources, but rather meaning that he came to a new understanding of Jesus as the Messiah. He acknowledged that Jesus Christ was really Lord, a radical change from that understanding necessary for the previous persecution in which he had been engaged. But the new understanding of Jesus was no more radical a change than the corresponding change in his understanding of himself. Only in this new situation does Paul know his own identity. This is what faith is.[13]

In the new understanding of self, there is the element of surrender. In the essay, "Grace and Freedom," Bultmann depicts the free act of decision on man's part as a surrender to God's grace in such a radical sense that it cannot look at or give an account of itself.[14] Man's faith is a precondition of receiving God's grace, but if it came other than by surrender, man would get the notion that he had fulfilled the conditions. Faith is the surrender to God's grace.[15]

Closely related to the idea of surrender, if not identical with it, is the idea that faith is renunciation. This element in man's new self-understanding is reflected in his renunciation

of self-glorying, works, self-sufficiency and world-sufficiency.
In fact, faith renounces all security, religious or otherwise,
as it turns solely and wholly to God.[16]

The new self-understanding of faith stresses the individual .
and inward nature of faith. Bultmann knows of no general
faith, only individual faith. It always happens to individuals
who act in decision to turn to God. As such, it can really be
discussed only as "my" faith in any given moment.[17] Subjec-
tivity is clearly the nature of faith to Bultmann.

Although faith's relation to the world has already been
noted, it is important to repeat that the new self-understanding
of faith involves "being-in-the-world" but not "of-the-world."
One understands himself as detached from the world. Bultmann repeatedly returned to Paul's phrase "as though not"
to describe this nonascetic detachment from the world. Both
Schubert Ogden[18] and Norman Perrin[19] take note of Bultmann's affinity for this phrase. Bultmann understands Paul to
mean that one lives in the world, engages in its business, etc.,
but lives "as though not" (1 Cor. 7:29–31) in the world.

When Bultmann describes faith as a new self-understanding, he does not mean the kind of understanding at which one
may arrive by means of study or reflection. It is the result of
an act of faith in response to God's act of grace.

FAITH AS AN ACT OF DECISION

Bultmann makes quite a distinction between an "act" and a
"work." Faith is an act and never a work. An act is the kind
of event in which I find my being. I enter into it and live in it.
In short, I am involved in an act. For instance, I enter love or
friendship, and in such acts I both give myself and attain
my own being.[20] In contrast, a "work" is just something I do.
I can remain outside of it, look back upon it, and perhaps be
proud of it. Faith is an act of decision by which I enter a
relationship with God, in which I am involved in my whole
existence. I do not stand outside faith and evaluate it, but in

the free act of decision I surrender myself to God. Bultmann interprets Paul's doctrine of justification in the light of this contrast. One who thinks he is justified by works of the Law stands outside and is prone to pride. Faith is a decisive act in which my existence is changed.

As an act of decision, faith is in response to God's prior act of grace in Christ. Bultmann does not extol faith in faith, but faith "in" Christ. My act is a free act of decision, when, as a sinner, I hear God's Word telling me that "I am a sinner and that God in Christ forgives my sins—and such faith is a *free act* of decision." [21] This obedient hearing of faith is the responsive act of man to God's act; hence it is possible to speak also of faith as obedience.

Another way of stressing faith as an act of decision is to say that God calls man to faith by the preaching of the Word. Bultmann denies to man the power to generate faith, which always arises only when God calls it forth. (Here he differs from Heidegger who believes that man has within himself the power to make the decision for authentic existence.) Consequently, faith is God's creation. Faith is not a natural event but a miraculous one. It is as if God crucified me and brought me to life again in the call to faith. That God is my Father and that I am his child are not insights gained by reflection; such faith is produced only as a "miraculous act of God." [22]

Therefore, it follows that faith is always an event which "happens" [23] as an act of God. To speak of faith as an event which happens guards against errors such as thinking of faith as doctrines to be believed, a state of consciousness, or even an act of God which happened once-for-all and has continuing benefits. Bultmann does not want to introduce an element of insecurity into the idea, but he thinks that faith must be understood, not in the linear sense, but in the punctiliar sense of an event that happens every time I stand in the presence of God as a sinner and respond to his grace. Faith is not something I have. If it were so, I would presume upon it. Faith occurs only in given moments of decision. To live authentically is to

be open to God's future in every moment. Bultmann would
have no interest in a set of eternal principles which one might
hold. Rather, he is concerned that in every moment man
choose God in his concrete existence.[24]

If faith is not an act performed once-for-all with enduring
results, neither is it a continuous act. It always happens in
specific moments as an act of God when man responds to
God.[25] Nothing is continuous. Certainly, faith is not. As an
act of decision, faith happens in specific moments of decision.
The commandment to love is not a general principle but a
command for specific moments. One loves only in specific
and concrete moments when decision so requires.[26]

As an event which happens, faith is also an eschatological
occurrence, because it is a response to God's Word in the
eschatological event of Christ, and it inaugurates eschatological existence for the individual who believes.[27]

FAITH AS OBEDIENCE

Faith is the "obedient hearing" of the Word.[28] Paul uses the
term "obedience" to tie together several significant emphases.
As obedience, faith is an act (Rom. 1:5; 16:19). To believe
in Christ is to accept the Christian kerygma and to acknowledge Jesus Christ as Lord. This is the surrender of one's self-
understanding and coming to a new self-understanding in
which there is no ground for boasting. One is now obedient to
Christ; he has chosen to be.[29] Bultmann sees obedience not in
the legalistic setting, but in the true Old Testament sense of
obeying God on the basis of choice, not coercion. Obedience
is one of the characteristics of faith in the New Testament
sense. In a brief dictionary article, Bultmann pointed out
that faith in the New Testament means to believe, obey, trust,
hope, and to be faithful. Specifically, it means that one ac-
cepts the kerygma, believes the contents of the gospel regard-
ing Christ's death and resurrection, personally trusts in
Christ, stands in the faith, and is faithful to what is believed.[30]

Faith in Christ involves obedience to God. Faith is a transforming act, and obedience by choice is a distinguishing mark of its genuineness. This shows the surrender and renunciation of the old self and its world and the joyful choice to have one's existence in Christ. Such obedience is a personal act of free decision.[31]

One does not come to faith in Christ and then decide whether or not he will obey. Such a dichotomy is inconceivable. Faith is the very act of obedience to God.

Faith as obedience makes Christian ethics an inseparable part of faith and not merely a likely, or positive, result of such faith. Bultmann argues that Paul said *"the decisive saving act of Christ is 'obedience' and 'love.'"*[32] Paul was not speaking about personality traits observable in the historical Jesus. Rather, he was speaking about the preexistent Christ whose obedience and love not only save us, but become known to us only in our hearing of the kerygma. Thereby we have the possibility of obedience and love. Bultmann's ethical teachings come to focus in the terms "radical obedience"[33] and "love" for one's neighbor in the concrete situations of life. But such ethical living is not an optional course for the person who by faith has come to authentic existence. Neither is such living a result of such faith. It is in fact an integral part of faith. Faith is obedience and love, and these are not qualities described in the abstract, but concrete realities in authentic existence.

FAITH AS FREEDOM

Bultmann likes to define faith as freedom, and therefore the subject of freedom is as important as the subject of faith. He has several specific articles on the subject[34] and constantly refers to freedom in his more general works. He says, "The genuine freedom of faith is man's radical surrender to God's grace as the sole means whereby he is saved from . . . his total lostness."[35] He sees Paul's interpretation of the new

eschatological existence in faith as freedom: (1) freedom
from sin, (2) freedom from the law, (3) freedom from men
and their standards (the world), and (4) freedom from
death.[36]

Inauthentic existence is bondage to sin. The obedient surrender to the grace of God brings liberation from sin and a
new self-understanding.[37] Freedom from sin is not merely
freedom from the guilt of sin, but is actually "release from
sinning," or release from the power of sin. Bultmann is not
thinking in terms of any sinless perfection, but is speaking of
freedom from the compulsion of sin.[38] Freedom from sin
involves a paradox in that it comes about only in a new bondage to Christ. Man becomes Christ's servant (Rom. 7:6; 1
Thess. 1:9; Rom. 14:18), but to be a slave of Christ is to be
Christ's "freedman" (1 Cor. 7:22).[39]

Faith is freedom from self. Sinful man's self-assertion has
ruled out faith and has intensified his fallenness by arranging
his existence around a false center. One cannot know authentic existence until he is delivered from himself. This is precisely what happened in Christ. Man was freed from himself
and from sin for God.[40]

Faith is freedom from the Law and for love. Although the
Law was good, it had become the "power of sin" (1 Cor.
15:56) for those not in faith. Christ was the "end of the law"
(Rom. 19:4) in that he brought freedom from its tyranny
(Gal. 2:4). But this liberty is not license. It is freedom to
love. Judaism had fallen into bondage to the Law, but Christian faith includes only free people. Sin had its seat of power
in the flesh and was awakened by the Law. Christ's act de-
stroyed both the power of sin and the Law. Men in faith, therefore, are free to live by the Spirit and not by the legalistic
letter (Gal. 5:18; Rom. 7:5f.).[41] Freedom from Law does not
invite antinomianism, even though all things are now lawful
for me (1 Cor. 6:12; 10:23), because all things are not
wholesome, and the man of faith is free and must not again
become a slave. The man of faith lives by love for his neigh-

bor. This love is Christ's kind of love and knows personal responsibility.[42]

Faith is freedom from the world. In sin, man was enslaved to the world. By faith, man comes to authentic existence under God the Creator, and the "world" is now "creation." In man's new self-understanding, the world is different. Instead of living in the false security of the world, man in his radical surrender to God is open for what God demands[43] and for what God sends.[44] Having been liberated from the world, Christians are citizens of a heavenly commonwealth (Phil. 3:20). They do not live on the basis of worldly things (Phil. 3:19). A certain unworldliness characterizes their existence (Heb. 13:13; Heb. 11:13; 1 Pet. 1:1, 2:11). But they are not ascetics withdrawn from the world. They are in the world (1 Cor. 5:10) and have been instructed to keep that particular situation in the world (1 Cor. 7:17). Slaves must remain as such (1 Cor. 7:21–24). The married and the unmarried must do the same (1 Cor. 7:26–28). "It is in this attitude of 'as though not' that Christian freedom from the world consists."[45]

Paul grasped this freedom from the world as the "as though not" more clearly than any other New Testament writer. It is reflected in 1 Peter 2:16, but Bultmann thinks that the idea was soon lost, and later New Testament writings show signs of an emerging schedule of behavior, like a legalistic religion. To Paul, the world had lost its power. Nothing was clean or unclean of itself (Rom. 14:14, 20; 1 Cor. 10:26). The man of faith has only one motive, love. He seeks the good of his neighbor (1 Cor. 10:24), and whether he drinks or refrains, it is all for the "glory of God" (1 Cor. 10:31). Such freedom from the world allows the man of faith to renounce even the right of claiming his freedom in order to decide in the interest of other men and even to become a slave in order to help men (1 Cor. 9:19).[46] Paul rejected asceticism, Gnostic libertinism, etc., and chose to live in-the-world "as though not."

Faith is freedom from death. Without faith man falls under

the power of sin and death. In faith man is freed from the power of sin and death. Freedom from death can mean the future apocalyptic expectation of resurrection from the dead, a present victory over death, or both.

While John prefers the present victory of life over death, Paul preserves both the future expectation and the present realization. The wages of sin is death (Rom. 6:23), but in faith men receive the free gift of eternal life. The last enemy of man which Christ will destroy is death (1 Cor. 15:20–27), but even in this future hope there is already a victory over death in that "I have been crucified with Christ . . . Christ . . . lives in me" (Gal. 2:20).[47]

However, freedom from death as victory over death is the existential quality of faith. We are "dead to sin and alive to God in Christ Jesus" (Rom. 6:11, 13). Christ's victory over death likewise solves the problem of suffering, in that I see my suffering in a new light.[48] Believing in Christ is to be crucified with him. In accepting the judgment of death existentially, man comes to the knowledge of his own nothingness and God's creative power to make him a new creation, now. In forgiving sin, God takes man from nothingness which is death and raises him up for new life.[49]

FAITH AS ESCHATOLOGICAL EXISTENCE

In the traditional use of theological language, eschatology designates the study of "last things" in the sense of a future consummation of history, death, resurrection, judgment, and final states. In his frequent use of the terms "eschatology," and "eschatological," Bultmann does not intend to convey the traditional understanding. He regards the saving event of Christ as the great eschatological event. Furthermore, he thinks that the preaching of that event is an eschatological event in that it calls men into an authentic existence which is an eschatological occurrence.

During the New Testament period, apocalyptic eschatologi-

cal thought was prevalent. In this type of thinking, characteristic of Daniel and Revelation and other passages (Mark 13;
Matt. 24–26) in the New Testament, the end of history was
expected to break in abruptly as an act of God. This conclusion would be quite fitting in a view of history which considered the world hopelessly evil. God would- simply call a
halt to it. Although Bultmann acknowledges the prevalence
of this view in the New Testament, he thinks that there is a
movement away from it to a more historical view of eschatology. He understands history as being made up of human decisions in freedom and that the focus is really personal history
rather than some futuristic apocalyptic scheme. If historicity
is really personal human existence, and if the New Testament
mythological language is as Bultmann thinks it is, then it is
natural that he would demythologize the language and see
eschatological themes in terms of personal existence.

In short, Bultmann thinks that authentic existence (faith)
is the fullness of eschatological existence in the present. Christ
brought a new situation for man. Existence in faith—freedom
from sin, the world, and death—is the essence of the eschatological hope. To be open to the future does not have reference to some date yet to come, but it expresses man's readiness
to be open to any "not yet" as God may call him to. Existence
in faith between the "no longer" and the "not yet" is historicity and eschatology.

Bultmann has felt free to demythologize New Testament
eschatology because he thinks that the process had already
begun in the New Testament itself—in John for instance—
and also that it is impossible for modern man to believe that
Christ will literally come on the clouds of heaven to complete
his redemptive work.[50] The primary sources in the New Testament are John and Paul. Bultmann entitles his discussion of
Paul's teaching on the subject, "Faith as Eschatological Occurrence,"[51] and of John's presentation, "Faith as Eschatological Existence."[52]

Although Paul retained the futuristic apocalyptic expecta-

tion, he emphasized that the greatest eschatological event had
already happened. Christ had brought an end to the old aeon
and had introduced the new.[53] In faith, man dies and is buried
with Christ in baptism and is also raised with him (Rom. 6:
3–11). Walking by the Spirit is eschatological existence now,
and a new creation.[54] This brings joy and peace. The believer
is a new creation (2 Cor. 5:17).[55]

Bultmann understands Paul to have viewed history as a
unity in Adam. In true apocalyptic fashion, Paul expected
the end of history, not as the result of historical events, but
as an abrupt breaking-off by God. But Bultmann detects a
modification in Paul stemming from his doctrine of man.
Paul recognized man's historicity, that man's existence is
history [56] in which his decisions open up the possibility for his
true being. Having heard God's call, man responds, lives in
freedom, loves his neighbor. His life is an existence "on the
way" or between the "no longer" and the "not yet." [57]

All of the present meaning of life in the Spirit can be found
in John's writings, but in different terminology. John dis-
missed the futuristic aspect of eschatology, according to Bultmann, and reduced eschatological hope to the present event of
Christ. The conversation with Martha indicates to Bultmann
that man does not look forward to a future hope of resurrection. Rather, instead of a resurrection at the "last day" (John
11:25), as Martha expected, Jesus told her, "I am the resurrection. . . ." [58]

If faith depends on an act of God in Christ, and if man
knows Christ only in his personal existence, the decisive event
is eschatological. "We must, therefore, say that to live in faith
is to live an eschatological existence, to live beyond the world,
to have passed from death to life." [59]

The unique element in the Christ event is not that he came
at one, and no other, point in history, but rather it is that the
particular event "Jesus Christ is to be understood as the
eschatological 'once for all'." [60]

If I understand Bultmann correctly, he does not speak

about what will come in the future. He thinks the future is God's and therefore not at man's disposal. Man is to be open to the future and to whatever God brings to him. This means being open to death, also. Existential faith does not consist of a statement of the content of future events, but rather it is "to be open to God's future in the face of death and darkness." [61]

His critics object that Bultmann's demythologizing destroys eschatology. There can be no doubt that it leaves little room for the customary eschatological themes. Bultmann replies that his eschatological thought exposes the New Testament meaning within existence to men who can no longer think in mythological ways. He thinks that his demythologizing shows the "character of faith as freedom for the future." [62]

X. Summary and Evaluation

Bultmann's influence and prominence continue. Even the theologians who differ with him find it necessary to come to terms with him while stating their own positions. Upon close examination, the term "post-Bultmannian" appears to be needlessly burdened with the prefix "post."

Several reasons account for his continued prominence. He has written voluminously; his works are of exceedingly high quality; his subjects have been those of crucial concern to his age. He came along at a time in history when men were asking serious questions about their own existence. He responded to these questions in relevant terms of authentic existence and personal decision. He advocated a transcendent kind of existence which is "in" but not "of" the world. It is not ascetic, but is decisive, involved, and committed. He came into a world dominated by scientific method; he accepted both that method and the attendant mentality to the full. He brought with him a rich heritage of Christian faith and a deep personal Christian commitment. He retained the best of liberalism; he helped to found a new theological movement. Early in his career he chose an approach to theology, a methodology, which he has faithfully and consistently followed.

The bibliography of Bultmann's writings is lengthy, and there are numerous books and articles about him and his writings. But his influence extends beyond the limits of his specific fields of New Testament and theology.

During the 1960s a number of theologians, all of them influenced by Dietrich Bonhoeffer, published works on the theme of the secularization of Christianity. Some of Bultmann's early comments appear to have anticipated Bonhoeffer. For instance, while interpreting Christian faith as an eschatological existence in the present, Bultmann stated that such an emphasis did not abandon nor threaten man's secular existence. He interpreted faith as a renunciation of the world in such a way that it was not ascetic and made no protest against the secular. Faith has no desire to take its eschatological community out of the secular world, and has no opposition toward secular science. Rather, Christian faith frees man not from but for the secular world. The Christian has a special interest in the secular world since it is here that he decides for his authentic existence.[1]

Bultmann is not famous for his writings in the field of ethics, but he has made a significant contribution to the present discussion of situation ethics. He did not develop a social ethic, but spoke of authentic existence in terms of individual responsible love for the neighbor under the demand of God. Both Bishop Robinson in *Honest To God* and Joseph Fletcher in *Situation Ethics* cited Bultmann and employed the same "love alone" guideline for ethics. Bultmann argued that man cannot predetermine what will be good or bad, but must obey God in each moment as it arrives. The norm is loving one's neighbor. Love is not an ethical principle, and a set of rules cannot be derived from it. The command to love does not deal with a system of ethics, but is a command for each present moment. One cannot even determine or choose who his neighbor will be. This is revealed only in the moment or situation of confrontation.[2] Fletcher refers to Bultmann as a situationist in theological ethics,[3] and seems to be enunciating ethics on the basis of Bultmann's theology.

BULTMANN'S METHODOLOGY

In general, the dialectical theologians, like Barth, have been somewhat unappreciative of the values of philosophy for theological method. Bultmann has contributed toward narrowing this gulf. By clearly identifying his approach in existentialism, Bultmann set his theology in clear perspective without surrendering theology to philosophy.

However, there are numerous criticisms of Bultmann's approach. He employed the existentialist analysis of the early Heidegger of *Sein und Zeit,* but the later Heidegger has moved in a different direction. Existentialism itself is so diverse and unsystematic that its suitability for theological method is debatable. Bultmann replies that in this analysis of existence he found a method of approach which does justice to New Testament interpretation. Furthermore, his interpretation has been shaped more by the New Testament than by Heidegger.

Demythologizing has made a significant contribution toward understanding the message of the New Testament. No one can deny the difficulty of trying to interpret the angels, demons, and the three-story universe of the New Testament to men who think in scientific terms. Nor can the thoughtful person refuse to be grateful to Bultmann. However, objections have been raised to his program of existentialist interpretation.[4] Perhaps the most serious criticism of Bultmann's method is the apparent inconsistency between two of his major assumptions.

Bultmann maintains (1) that existentialist analysis accurately describes the possibility of man's authentic existence, but (2) authentic existence can only be realized actually by faith in the Christ of historical event.[5] Ogden maintains that Bultmann's theology is "shot through with an inconsistency that completely determines its basic structure and movement."[6] It is awkward to acknowledge the clear insight of existentialist analysis into the true nature of existence, but to affirm at the same time that one cannot know such authentic existence except on the basis of the historical event of Christ. His critics maintain that Bultmann has retained the central "myth" of the New Testament on the basis of theological or traditional grounds, in spite of the fact that his own method and definition of myth would "demythologize" God and his act.

Bultmann is the embodiment of a radical historical-critical method of biblical study. Of itself, this is not bad. However, some of his assumptions (or conclusions) in the form-criticism study of the Gospels are contrary to generally accepted historical knowledge. It is true that the Gospels are primarily about faith; they are not intended to be scientific history. However, the assumption that the chronological, biographical, and geographical notes are editorial, and hence unreliable, is debatable. Even when the later dates are accepted for the writing of the synoptic Gospels, it is likely that eyewitnesses would still have been living who could have prevented inaccurate editorial additions to the narratives. Bultmann asserted that we know practically nothing historical about Jesus. Günther Bornkamm's *Jesus of Nazareth*,[7] for instance, written in Bultmann's own method of study, maintains that we know quite a few historical facts about Jesus. Bultmann appraises rather highly the *Sitz im Leben* as an influential factor in shaping the narratives in the Gospels. He may have overlooked or obscured the fact that one of the needs of the community was knowledge about what Jesus did and said just because he was Jesus.

Otto Michel criticized Bultmann for making Paul's theology the norm within the canon and for placing the Gospels in the margin. He thought that Bultmann in his interpretation removed the authority of Jesus of Nazareth as the norm and replaced it with the unfolding of the human spirit. In his judgment, the whole Word of God is at stake.[8]

A serious question about Bultmann's methodology is that

self-understanding becomes normative for theological statements. This self-understanding is individualistic and needs
the corrective discipline of history and the community.

FAITH IN EXISTENTIALIST PERSPECTIVE

When Christian faith is interpreted solely in terms of human
existence, there are noticeable advantages and also short-
comings.

Existence is always under the demand of God, but God is
known only in terms of existence. This requires the understanding of God in terms of personal existential encounter.
Therefore, we speak "of" God but cannot speak "about" God
lest we construct an idol. However, since we cannot compare
notes and say what God means to us, are we not consigned to
an individualistic interpretation of God which may be idola-
try, too? Bultmann speaks of God as Creator and holy, but
these terms are in his biblical tradition. His method of interpretation requires him to say that speaking of God as Creator
means only that "I understand myself to be a creature which
owes its existence to God." [9]

When he is criticized for reducing God to subjective existence, Bultmann emphatically denies that this is his intention
or a necessary result of his method. Yet, we can still say only
that God is; we cannot say *what* God is like. But if we can
know *that* God is on the basis of human existence, why can we
not know at least something of *what* God is? Christians have
agreed after centuries of discussion of the New Testament
material that we can say some rather definite things about
what God is like. If we rule these affirmations out on the basis
of our method, is it not just as reasonable to conclude that
the affirmation *that* God is, is also an illusion?

Human existence is worldly, being-in-the-world; the world
is this world. Consequently, the eschatological hope of the
New Testament must be interpreted as a dimension of this-
worldly existence. Therefore eschatology loses its futuristic

element and is reduced to the present quality of existence. Traditional Christian hope grounded in Christ and the New Testament records has always included a strong conviction that God has something more for his people beyond death. One can build a strong case for this hope. If God is the Beyond in our midst, and if eschatological existence brings this element into the present, is it necessary to omit the Beyond in the beyond?

Existence is historical. Man is historicity; he lives only in history; he has his own personal history, and is at the mercy of history. Bultmann's understanding of existence as historical adds an important dimension to life in one's own time. The understanding of one's personal history and the acknowledgement of responsibility for it stress correctly the biblical teaching on man's responsibility. However, the present moment of history is exaggerated so much that one is likely to overlook the fact that previous history bequeaths to man a legacy of great value. In choosing authentic existence in a particular historical moment, does one not stand as the heir of a historical past? Does not the inordinate concern for my own personal history border on ingratitude? Does not my failure to acknowledge this "plus" suggest that when I make my choice I am operating on borrowed capital without paying interest? Furthermore, in spite of its exciting sound, does not "openness to the future" borrow unwittingly from the past? What is "openness to the future" if not related to the idea of destiny? Does not destiny stand in a position of indebtedness to history?

The uniqueness of existence is the potentiality which stands before man in his moments of decision. This sounds encouragingly similar to Jesus' demand for discipleship, but there are other implications. The constant accentuation of the moment of decision stresses a view of existence which is intermittent and not continuous. It appears to be severed from the past and future. Christian faith stresses the enduring character of existence. The demand to follow Christ up the narrow road is not the last decision to be made, but in the New Testament it

appears to be a decision within which subsequent decisions
will be made. Does not this view of existence move away from
the continuous and enduring stability expected of faith in the
New Testament?

Even potentiality, while stressing opportunity for the future, tends to diminish one's personal history. Does not the
person who repeatedly chooses authentic existence build up or
accumulate something which abides? Has he not already
achieved authentic character to some degree? Is everything
risked with each new decision?

Existence is individual; individuals make decisions and
gain or lose authentic existence. Some of the most serious
implications for Bultmann's theology grow out of this individualistic understanding of existence. For instance, in addition to the limit on what I can say of God, there is a serious
lack of social ethics and a minimal emphasis on the church.[10]

Bultmann correctly interpreted Jesus as not advocating a
theory of social or individual ethics. Rather, Jesus taught
that man should obey God and love his neighbor.[11] But Bultmann went further and maintained that Jesus saw man as
insecure before that which confronted him in each new moment. It is true that Jesus had no set of rules, but Bultmann
maintains that belief in God is stifled by living together with
other persons, and such living together presents a danger "of
losing its real character as a community of free and isolated
persons, and of deteriorating into a clamour of voices weak-
ening us and deceiving us about our solitariness. . . ."[12] Bultmann continued to show how individual man could lose his
individualistic existence in the community. This excessive
stress on the individual's existence does less than justice to
the New Testament idea of loving the neighbor. An isolated
self is not necessarily spared the arrogance and false security
which befall those who get lost in the community. It is quite
difficult to see how one can make responsible decisions in
loving the neighbor and at the same time remain an isolated
self.

The exaggerated individualism of Bultmann neglects the doctrine of the church. Macquarrie noted with amazement that Bultmann's two-volume *Theology of the New Testament* discusses nearly one hundred fifty Greek terms but omits the word *koinonia*.[13] Of course, Bultmann does not completely ignore the church. He is a churchman and has contributed significantly to the church of his day. He interpreted Paul's view of the church as a community of the faithful called of God and constituted by the Word. Paul saw the church as a continuation of the Christ event, the body of Christ.[14] It is a community, but in essence is invisible,[15] an eschatological community whose members have already been taken out of the world.

This minimal emphasis on the doctrine of the church is rather astonishing. The proclamation of the kerygma is very important to Bultmann; only the church makes this proclamation. In the New Testament, faith comes about by hearing the proclaimed Word and results in an involvement with other believers. The New Testament believers shared their lives, dangers, hopes, and even their property. This witnessing community is always a part of the proclaiming event. Does not this witness contribute materially to the credibility of the assertions and challenge of the gospel? Does not such witness have a bearing on the individual's pre-understanding and self-understanding? Today, when a person hears this gospel proclaimed calling him to faith, does he hear it as an isolated individual or one in the context of a community of faith which helps him understand the choice before him?

FAITH AND HISTORY

In spite of the difficulty of translation into English, Bultmann's distinction between *Historie* and *Geschichte* is helpful. His view that *Historie* is a closed cause-effect continuum is in keeping with modern scientific understanding of history; his view that *Geschichte* is personal meaningful history whose

events continue to impinge on man's life is in keeping with
the nature of the biblical events. However, Bultmann's discussions of the relationship between faith and *Historie* are not
altogether satisfactory.

He is correct in his refusal to permit faith to walk with the
crutch of historical validation. Faith is best understood as
existential. But, is he correct in separating so completely
Christian faith and the historical events in which it had its
origin? Biblical faith is distinct from most other religions
precisely because of its grounding in historical events. The
exodus of the Hebrews from Egypt is a clear example. He-
brew faith did not hinge on the ability to verify the exact date
or number of persons involved. It is also true that Egyptian
observers did not see God's hand nor hear God's Word in the
event. Faith is subjective and existential. However, the Hebrews looked back to the exodus both for its *Historie* and its
Geschichte. It is quite inconceivable that they could have
been indifferent to the historical event and its details as Bultmann is toward the historical Jesus.

One of the most frequent criticisms of Bultmann is that he
has ignored the continuity between the historical Jesus and
the Christ of faith.[16] The early Christians possessed some
knowledge of the historical Jesus. They regarded this Jesus
and the Christ of faith to be one and the same. Even though
we may not be able to know very completely the Jesus of history, what is known is of more importance to historical men
than Bultmann's viewpoint seems to allow. Faith does not
have to await historical verification, but men of faith are also
historical creatures; they ask questions of history and are
thereby historically limited. The existential faith of the disciples may have inherited more from the historical events than
they or we know.

CHRIST, CHRISTOLOGY, AND GOD

Much of Bultmann's discussion of Christ and God is quite
helpful. We speak "of" God in terms of existential acquaint-

ance and reverence. We avoid speaking "about" God as if he were an object, or as if we stood outside in a neutral position. We confess that our only claim to know God is based on his act in the event of Christ. This builds on the right foundation. We believe that faith emerges from decisive response to hearing the proclaimed message of Christ. So, faith is both an act of God and an act of man in which man comes to authentic existence. The grace of God was manifested in the unique historical event of Christ through whose cross and resurrection God has delivered us from sin, slavery, world, and death for faith, freedom, and life in the Spirit. Christ is the Word of God and the revelation of God, and is always contemporary in the proclamation.

Bultmann's critics have found cause to criticize him for what has been omitted in the foregoing summary. He has reduced most of what is said about Jesus Christ to the existential encounter of faith. But he believes in and proclaims more about God than can be affirmed by his own method. This raises the question as to whether he can pass on to his generation and the next as much as he received from the generation previous to his own. The affirmation that only the individual knows God existentially and that nothing can be said "about" God gives some basis for the criticism that God has been reduced to the level of subjective existence.

Throughout history, Christian faith has made affirmations in the realm of Christology as to what Christ disclosed about the nature of God. But, Bultmann does not include Chalcedonian Christology in his theology. He does not speak about the deity of Christ—only that God acted in him. To him, resurrection and ascension are existential events in the realm of personal faith. Then, can we even say that "God is love"? If so, what does it mean? It cannot mean that Christ, God's Son, displayed the quality of love in his earthly life so that we have an insight into God's nature as love. It can only mean that in faith I existentially know a release from bondage which I call the forgiveness of sins.

So, Christ does not add to man's knowledge about God, but

rather, calls men to faith in God. While the writers of the
New Testament were primarily concerned with this existential
trust in God, as is Bultmann, it seems to me that they considered Jesus to have disclosed God to them so that some meaningful statements could be made about his nature.[17] Theology
is talking about God. Christian theology has talked about
God as revealed in Jesus Christ. Bultmann's method of existentialist interpretation severely limits what can be said.

FAITH AS AUTHENTIC EXISTENCE

Bultmann's greatest theological clarification is his interpretation of faith which he contrasts to the life of sin and inauthentic existence. Man without faith lives in unbelief, surrender to the world, slavery, and death. But, when man hears
the proclamation of Christ's kerygma and chooses to respond,
faith happens. Faith brings a radical transformation in one's
self-understanding and attitude toward the world; it brings
freedom from sin, the Law, and death. Then, the man in faith
joyfully obeys God and loves his neighbor as he expectantly
looks to the future.

There are some objections to this interpretation. The new
self-understanding threatens to eclipse a new understanding
of God. Certainly, a new self-understanding is one part of
New Testament repentance and faith, and a very important
part. But, is not this secondary to, and a result of, the primary
change in understanding God? Repentance is pointed toward
God, faith toward the Lord Jesus Christ (Acts 20:21). One
cannot easily avoid the suspicion that faith in terms of one's
own existence tends to get pointed toward man instead of
toward God. Much can be said for the New Testament idea
that repentance is forgetting self, or denying self (Matt. 16:
24), and turning to God.

Faith is accurately described in terms of an act (a deed in
which one is deeply involved instead of a superficial work) of
decision. It helps to think of faith as something which happens as an event. But, when Bultmann couples this decisive

act with his view of existence as being made up of these decisions, one gets an idea of brokenness, or repeatedness, rather
than growth in patience and endurance.

Faith as obedience, radical obedience, is a helpful insight.
It would be doubly helpful if it were more closely related to
an understanding of what God is like. However, since I do not
know what God is like, I cannot understand obedience as
compliance with His will. Obedience is not to the Law. Obedience is united with love. I live obediently under God and
love my neighbor as both he and his needs are revealed to me
in the situations which come.

Faith as eschatological existence says something very meaningful about Christian life. The whole urgency of eternity is
compressed into the decisive and responsible decisions and
acts of historical moments. The spirit of the New Testament
call to discipleship is captured in this view. Jesus spoke to
men telling them to forsake all else and to follow him. Some
of them followed, sensing the eternal within the temporal.
John wrote that to know God and Christ is life eternal (17:3).
But, history can be cruel and tragic. Countless millions in
every age, including the New Testament age, are exploited,
enslaved, robbed, and killed in wars and by diseases. Many
of them were denied the choice for authentic existence, or
scarcely got the chance to exist at all. Biblical faith is sat-
urated with the hope that since God is the Creator and Judge,
beyond this life there is something in store for man. This hope
does not weaken the interpretation of faith as eschatological
existence now. Nor does it encourage irresponsible decision
or indecision. Rather, it stands as an assurance of the genuineness of faith now. Bultmann's silence on this subject is
consistent with his method. But, the silence raises a question
about his method.

Science has changed modern man's view of the world and
history. Bultmann is in full agreement with this new outlook.
He is also a profound Christian thinker who has attempted to
translate Christian faith into the language of modern, secular
man. His effort is both significant and relevant. He has dealt

with the right questions. He has left us all in his debt.

One other question deserves consideration. Can Bultmann's method of interpretation pass on the Christian kerygma to the next generation?

John Macquarrie employs an illustration in discussing Bultmann's treatment of the Gospels which may be applicable. He compared the Gospel record to a ladder by which men climb upon a higher level of understanding. Having climbed upon the roof by means of the ladder, one may kick the ladder away or leave it in place. Obviously, kicking it away has some advantages. It manifests one's confidence that he can remain permanently and intends to do so. But, if left in place, the ladder could have some further usefulness. One may wish to explain to others how he got on the roof, or to show them how they may make the ascent. Macquarrie suggested that, at first sight, Bultmann's demythologizing program appeared to kick the ladders away rather freely.[18]

Bultmann is very interested in the proclamation, and in making the Christian message intelligible to modern men. Explaining to others why one believes in Christ or how he came to stand in faith is crucial for Bultmann's purpose. It appears to me that Bultmann has overcorrected in trying to avoid making history a crutch for faith. The historical ladder was there, and perhaps it has considerably more value for faith than Bultmann thinks. However, Bultmann's interpretation is exciting in that it suggests that we can have authentic existence by this existential faith in Christ right now.

Perhaps, if Christians responded in this way and made responsible decisions of love for neighbors, the task of making the Christian message intelligible would not be so difficult. Men outside of faith might respond much more readily to such examples of authentic existence than to a clear historical description of the ladder by which we ascended to faith. The crucial test is whether one is defending an abandoned ladder or living on the plane of authentic existence. Bultmann speaks as a man who has chosen authenticity—Christian faith.

Footnotes

CHAPTER I

1. Rudolf Bultmann, *Existence and Faith*, trans. Schubert M. Ogden (Cleveland and New York: World Publishing Company, 1960).
2. Ibid., p. 286.   3. Ibid., p. 288.   4. Ibid., p. 165.
5. Walter Schmithals, *An Introduction to the Theology of Rudolf Bultmann*, trans. John Bowden (London: SCM Press Ltd., 1968), pp. 296–99.
6. For bibliographies see Charles W. Kegley, ed., *The Theology of Rudolf Bultmann* (New York: Harper & Row, 1966), pp. 289–310; Norman Perrin, *The Promise of Bultmann* (Philadelphia and New York: J. B. Lippincott Company, 1969), pp. 110–116; and Schmithals, op. cit., pp. 325–28.
7. Adolf Harnack, *What Is Christianity?* trans. Thomas Bailey Saunders (New York: Harper & Bros., 1957), pp. vii–xviii.
8. Rudolf Bultmann, *Primitive Christianity in Its Contemporary Setting*, trans. R. H. Fuller (Cleveland and New York: World Publishing Company, 1956).
9. Rudolf Bultmann and Karl Kundsin, *Form Criticism: Two Essays on New Testament Research*, trans. Frederick C. Grant (New York: Harper & Bros., 1962); Rudolf Bultmann, *The History of the Synoptic Tradition*, trans. John Marsh (Oxford: Basil Blackwell, 1963).
10. See footnote 9.
11. Karl Barth, *The Epistle to the Romans*, trans. Edwyn C. Hoskyns (London: Oxford University Press, 1933). The original commentary appeared in German in 1918, but it was the revised edition of 1921 which sparked the New Reformation emphasis known as dialectical theology.

12. Rudolf Bultmann, *Faith and Understanding*, I, trans. Louise Pettibone Smith (New York and Evanston: Harper & Row, 1969), p. 29.

13. Ibid., p. 30   14. Ibid., pp. 32f.   15. Ibid., p. 146.

16. Ibid., p. 163.

17. Rudolf Bultmann, "New Testament and Mythology," *Kerygma and Myth*, ed. Hans Werner Bartsch, trans. Reginald H. Fuller (London: S.P.C.K., 1960).

18. Rudolf Bultmann, *Jesus and the Word*, trans. Louise Pettibone Smith and Erminie Huntress Lantero (New York: Charles Scribner's Sons, 1958).

19. Rudolf Bultmann, *Theology of the New Testament*, trans. Kendrick Grobel, 2 vols. (New York: Charles Scribner's Sons, 1951, 1955).

20. Rudolf Bultmann, *Das Evangelium des Johannes* (Göttingen: Vandenhoeck & Ruprecht, 1941). *The Gospel of John, A Commentary*, trans. G. R. Beasley-Murray (Philadelphia: The Westminster Press, 1971).

21. Rudolf Bultmann, "What Sense Is There to Speak of God?" *The Christian Scholar* 43 (1960), 213–22. This essay also appears as "What Does It Mean to Speak of God?" in *Faith and Understanding*, I.

22. Rudolf Bultmann, "The Idea of God and Modern Man," in Ronald Gregor Smith, ed., *The World Come of Age* (Philadelphia: Fortress Press, 1967).

23. Martin Heidegger, *Being and Time*, trans. John Macquarrie and Edward Robinson (New York: Harper & Bros., 1962).

24. Schmithals, op. cit., p. 15.

CHAPTER II

1. Bultmann, *Faith and Understanding*, I, 29.

2. Bultmann, *Existence and Faith*, pp. 92f.

3. Rudolf Bultmann, *Jesus Christ and Mythology* (New York: Charles Scribner's Sons, 1958), p. 74; see also Schmithals, op. cit., pp. 67ff.

4. Bultmann, "New Testament and Mythology," p. 24.

5. Ibid., p. 194.

6. Heidegger, op. cit. For the best comparison of Heidegger and Bultmann see John Macquarrie, *An Existentialist Theology* (New York and Evanston: Harper & Row, 1955); also David E. Roberts, "Heidegger," in *Existentialism and Religious Beliefs*, ed. Roger Hazelton (London, Oxford, and New York: Oxford University Press, 1957).

7. Macquarrie, op. cit., p. 13.   8. Heidegger, op. cit., p. 70.

9. Ibid., p. 78; Macquarrie, op. cit., p. 33.

10. Heidegger, op. cit., pp. 78ff.

11. Ibid., p. 80; Macquarrie, op. cit., p. 38.

12. Macquarrie, op. cit., p. 39.

13. Heidegger, op. cit., pp. 225ff.; Macquarrie, op. cit., pp. 112f.

14. Heidegger, op. cit., pp. 383ff.

15. Macquarrie, op. cit., p. 160.   16. Ibid., pp. 82ff.

17. Heidegger, op. cit., pp. 221-23.

18. Ibid., pp. 279–311.

19. Bultmann, *Existence and Faith*, pp. 92–110.

20. Rudolf Bultmann, *Essays: Philosophical and Theological*, trans. James C. G. Greig (London: SCM Press Ltd., 1955), pp. 67–89 (hereafter referred to as *Essays*).

21. Rudolf Bultmann, "The Significance of the Old Testament for the Christian Faith," in B. W. Anderson, ed., *The Old Testament and Christian Faith* (New York: Harper & Row; London: SCM Press, 1963), pp. 8–35.

22. Bultmann, "The Idea of God and Modern Man," pp. 256–73.

23. Rudolf Bultmann, *The Presence of Eternity, History and Eschatology* (New York: Harper & Bros., 1957) (hereafter referred to as *Presence*).

24. Bultmann, *Essays*, pp. 119–32.

25. Bultmann, *Presence*, pp. 95ff.; see also Bultmann, "The Significance of the Old Testament for the Christian Faith," p. 20.

26. Bultmann, *Essays*, p. 79.

27. Ibid., p. 81.   28. Ibid., p. 85.   29. Ibid., pp. 88f.

30. Bultmann, *Faith and Understanding*, I, 163.

31. Bultmann, *Existence and Faith*, p. 222.

32. Bultmann, *Faith and Understanding*, I, 46.

33. Bultmann, *Existence and Faith*, pp. 171ff.

34. Bultmann, *Faith and Understanding*, I, 168.

35. Ibid., pp. 166f.

36. Bultmann, "Bultmann Replies to His Critics," *Kerygma and Myth*, p. 199.

37. Bultmann, *Faith and Understanding*, I, 160.

38. Bultmann, *Presence*, pp. 1ff.

39. Perrin, *The Promise of Bultmann*, pp. 43f.

40. Bultmann, *Existence and Faith*, p. 102.

41. Ibid., p. 107.

42. Bultmann, *Essays*, pp. 125f.

CHAPTER III

1. Heinrich Ott, "Rudolf Bultmann's Philosophy of History," in Charles W. Kegley, ed., *The Theology of Rudolf Bultmann* (New York: Harper & Row, 1966), p. 51.

2. Martin Kähler, *The So-Called Historical Jesus and the Historic Biblical Christ* (Philadelphia: Fortress Press, 1964); the original German edition was published in 1892. See also, Bultmann, *Kerygma and Myth*, p. 82.

3. Bultmann, *Kerygma and Myth*.

4. Carl E. Braaten and Roy H. Harrisville, trans. and eds., *The Historical Jesus and the Kerygmatic Christ* (New York and Nashville: Abingdon Press, 1964), pp. 96f.; R. H. Fuller, "Translator's Preface," *Kerygma and Myth*, pp. xi-xii.

5. Perrin, op. cit., pp. 38f.

6. Albert Schweitzer, *The Quest of the Historical Jesus*, trans. W. Montgomery (New York: The Macmillan Company, 1948).

7. Perrin, op. cit., p. 43   8. Bultmann, *Presence*, p. 1.

9. Ibid., p. 11.   10. Ott, op. cit., p. 52.

11. Bultmann, *Presence*, p. 12.   12. Ibid., p. 24.

13. Ibid., p. 25.   14. Ibid., p. 29.   15. Ibid., p. 31.

16. Ibid., p. 37.   17. Ibid., p. 40.   18. Ibid., p. 43.

19. Ibid., p. 57.

20. R. G. Collingwood, *The Idea of History* (New York: Oxford University Press, 1956).

21. Ibid., p. 131.   22. Ibid., p. 133.

23. Bultmann, *Presence*, p. 119.   24. Kegley, op. cit., p. 278.

25. Bultmann, "New Testament and Mythology," p. 22.

CHAPTER IV

1. Bultmann, *Faith and Understanding*, I, 237.

2. Sören Kierkegaard, *Philosophical Fragments*, trans. David F. Swenson (Princeton: Princeton University Press, 1936), p. 87.

3. James M. Robinson, *The New Quest of the Historical Jesus* (Naperville, Ill.: Alec R. Allenson, 1959), p. 26.

4. Schweitzer, op. cit.   5. Robinson, op. cit., pp. 27f.

6. Ibid., p. 31.

7. Charles M. Sheldon, *In His Steps*, reprint edition (Philadelphia and Chicago: The John C. Winston Company, 1937).

8. Kähler, op. cit.

9. Bultmann, *Faith and Understanding*, I, 220ff.

10. Robinson, op. cit.

11. Rudolf Bultmann, "The Primitive Christian Kerygma and the Historical Jesus," in Braaten and Harrisville, op. cit., pp. 15–42. James M. Robinson thinks that Bultmann has moved somewhat with the "new quest" (*The New Quest of the Historical Jesus*, p. 21), but concedes Bultmann's opposition to it in James M. Robinson and John B. Cobb, eds., *The New Hermeneutic* (New York, Evanston, and London: Harper & Row, 1964), p. 61.

12. Bultmann, *Faith and Understanding*, I, 264.

13. Bultmann, *Jesus and the Word*, p. 8.

14. Ian Henderson, *Rudolf Bultmann* (London: Lutterworth Press, 1965), p. 14.

15. Bultmann, *History of the Synoptic Tradition*, pp. 1–7.

16. Bultmann, *Faith and Understanding*, I, 220f.

17. Ibid., p. 239.   18. Ibid., p. 241.

19. Bultmann, *Theology of the New Testament*, I, 3.

20. Schmithals, op. cit., p. 216.

21. Ibid.   22. Ibid., p. 212.

23. Bultmann, *Faith and Understanding*, I, 179.

24. Schmithals, loc. cit.

25. Rudolf Bultmann, "The Primitive Christian Kerygma and the Historical Jesus," p. 18.

CHAPTER V

1. Bultmann, "New Testament and Mythology," *Kerygma and Myth*, pp. 1–44.

2. Schmithals, op. cit., p. 250.

3. Rudolf Bultmann, *Jesus Christ and Mythology*.

4. Bultmann, "New Testament and Mythology," p. 10.

5. Ibid., pp. 10f.   6. Ibid.

7. Bultmann, *Jesus Christ and Mythology*, p. 19.

8. Bultmann, "New Testament and Mythology," p. 4.

9. Ibid., p. 5.

10. Bultmann, *Jesus Christ and Mythology*, pp. 14f.

11. Bultmann, "New Testament and Mythology," p. 9.

12. Ibid., p. 11.   13. Bultmann, *Essays*, p. 19.

14. Bultmann, "New Testament and Mythology," pp. 22ff.

15. Ibid., p. 26.   16. Ibid., p. 33.   17. Ibid., p. 35.

18. Ibid., p. 42.

19. Bultmann, *Jesus Christ and Mythology*, pp. 61ff.

20. Ibid., p. 62.   21. Ibid., pp. 35ff.

22. Schmithals, op. cit., p. 257.

23. Bultmann, *Jesus Christ and Mythology*, p. 70.

24. Ibid., p. 73.   25. Ibid., p. 82.   26. Ibid., p. 79.

27. Carl Michalson, *Worldly Theology* (New York: Charles Scribner's Sons, 1967), pp. 75ff.

28. Ibid., p. 77.

CHAPTER VI

1. Bultmann, "Bultmann Replies to His Critics," p. 192.

2. Bultmann, *Faith and Understanding*, I, p. 146.

3. Ibid., p. 29.

4. Bultmann, *Existence and Faith*, pp. 171ff.

5. Ibid., p. 174.   6. Ibid., p. 179.   7. Ibid., pp. 23f.

8. Bultmann, *Faith and Understanding*, I, 28ff.

9. Ibid., p. 40.   10. Bultmann, *Presence*, pp. 96ff.

11. Bultmann, *Existence and Faith*, p. 96.

12. Bultmann, *Essays*, p. 107.   13. Ibid., p. 118.

14. Bultmann, *Existence and Faith*, p. 59.

15. Ibid., p. 75.

16. Bultmann, *Faith and Understanding*, I, 249.

17. Ibid., p. 254.   18. Henderson, op. cit., pp. 36f.

19. Bultmann, *Jesus Christ and Mythology*, pp. 60–85.

20. Bultmann, "Bultmann Replies to His Critics," p. 196.

21. Bultmann, *Theology of the New Testament*, I, 22–26.

22. Bultmann, *Faith and Understanding*, I, 53–65.

23. Bultmann, "The Idea of God and Modern Man," pp. 256–73.

24. Bultmann, *Faith and Understanding*, I, 55.

25. Ibid., pp. 54f.

26. Ibid., p. 55; Rudolf Bultmann, *Existence and Faith*, pp. 94ff.

27. Schmithals, op. cit., p. 33.

28. Bultmann, "The Idea of God and Modern Man," p. 265.

29. Bultmann, *Faith and Understanding*, I, 65.

CHAPTER VII

1. Bultmann, "Bultmann Replies to His Critics," p. 221.

2. Ibid., p. 14.   3. Ibid., p. 196.   4. Ibid., p. 31.

5. Bultmann, *Faith and Understanding*, I, 254.

6 Bultmann, "Bultmann Replies to His Critics," p. 197.

7. Ibid.   8. Ibid., p. 35.

9. Bultmann, *Faith and Understanding*, I, 220ff.

10. Bultmann, *Theology of the New Testament*, I, 292ff.

11. Ibid.   12. Ibid.
13. Bultmann, *Faith and Understanding*, I, 241.
14. Bultmann, *Theology of the New Testament*, I, 302.
15. Bultmann, *Essays*, pp. 36ff.
16. Bultmann, "New Testament and Mythology," p. 39.
17. Bultmann, *Theology of the New Testament*, I, 295.
18. Bultmann, *Faith and Understanding*, I, 137.
19. Bultmann, *Theology of the New Testament*, I, 305.
20. Bultmann, *Faith and Understanding*, I, 308.
21. Rudolf Bultmann, "The Concept of the Word of God in the New Testament," ibid., pp. 286–312.
22. Ibid., p. 287.   23. Ibid., p. 298.   24. Ibid., p. 308.
25. Bultmann, *Theology of the New Testament*, I, 307.
26. Bultmann, *Existence and Faith*, p. 139.
27. Bultmann, *Theology of the New Testament*, II, 9.
28. Schmithals, op. cit., p. 152.
29. Bultmann, *Theology of the New Testament*, II, 58.
30. Ibid., p. 37.   31. Ibid., p. 58.
32. Ibid., p. 67; Bultmann, *Existence and Faith*, pp. 85, 78.
33. Bultmann, *Existence and Faith*, p. 59.
34. Ibid., p. 72.   35. Ibid., p. 75.
36. Bultmann, *Faith and Understanding*, I, 170f.
37. Bultmann, *Essays*, p. 118.

CHAPTER VIII

1. Bultmann, *Faith and Understanding*, I, 169.
2. Bultmann, *Existence and Faith*, p. 154.
3. Bultmann, *Faith and Understanding*, I, loc. cit.
4. Bultmann, *Theology of the New Testament*, I, 192.
5. Ibid., p. 127.
6. Rudolf Bultmann, "Christ the End of the Law," *Essays*, pp. 36–66.
7. Ibid., p. 47.
8. Bultmann, *Existence and Faith*, p. 190.
9. Bultmann, *Faith and Understanding*, I, 171.
10. Bultmann, *Existence and Faith*, p. 217.
11. Ibid., p. 216.   12. Ibid., pp. 216f., 255.   13. Ibid., p. 81.
14. Bultmann, *Theology of the New Testament*, I, 229ff.
15. Ibid., p. 232.   16. Ibid., p. 241.   17. Ibid., p. 242.
18. Bultmann, *Theology of the New Testament*, II, 15.
19. Rudolf Bultmann, *This World and the Beyond*, trans. Harold

Knight (New York: Charles Scribner's Sons, 1960), pp. 61f.
20. Bultmann, *Theology of the New Testament*, I, 246.
21. Ibid., p. 243.
22. Bultmann, *Theology of the New Testament*, II, 16.
23. Bultmann, *Theology of the New Testament*, I, 246.
24. Ibid.
25. John Macquarrie, *An Existentialist Theology* (New York and Evanston: Harper & Row, 1955), p. 122.

CHAPTER IX

1. Bultmann, *Theology of the New Testament*, I, 315.
2. Bultmann, *Faith and Understanding*, I, 117.
3. Bultmann, *Theology of the New Testament*, I, 314–24.
4. Ibid., p. 317.   5. Ibid., p. 319.   6. Ibid.
7. Ibid., pp. 322f.
8. Bultmann, *Faith and Understanding*, I, 275.
9. Ibid., p. 156.
10. Bultmann, *Jesus Christ and Mythology*, pp. 73f.
11. Bultmann, "New Testament and Mythology," p. 30.
12. Bultmann, *Essays*, pp. 45ff.
13. Bultmann, *Faith and Understanding*, I, 236.
14. Rudolf Bultmann, "Grace and Freedom," *Essays*, p. 176.
15. Ibid., p. 173.
16. Ibid., pp. 59, 176; see also Bultmann, "The Significance of the Old Testament for the Christian Faith," p. 26.
17. Bultmann, *Essays*, pp. 15f.
18. Schubert M. Ogden, "Introduction," Bultmann, *Existence and Faith*, p. 20.
19. Norman Perrin, *The Promise of Bultmann* (Philadelphia and New York: J. B. Lippincott Company, 1969), p. 73.
20. Bultmann, *Essays*, pp. 175f.
21. Bultmann, *Faith and Understanding*, I, 132.
22. Ibid., p. 47.   23. Ibid., p. 52.
24. Bultmann, *Existence and Faith*, p. 222; "The Significance of the Old Testament for the Christian Faith," p. 19.
25. Bultmann, *Faith and Understanding*, I, 50.
26. Bultmann, *Existence and Faith*, loc. cit.
27. Rudolf Bultmann, "Faith," in *Theological Dictionary of the New Testament*, trans. and ed. Geoffrey W. Bromiley (Grand Rapids: Wm. B. Eerdmans Publishing Company, 1968), VI, 220.
28. Bultmann, *Faith and Understanding*, I, 132.

29. Bultmann, *Theology of the New Testament*, I, 315.

30. Bultmann, "Faith," pp. 205–15.

31. Bultmann, *Essays*, p. 174.

32. Bultmann, *Faith and Understanding*, I, 246; note Phil. 2:6; 2 Cor. 8:9; Rom. 5:18, 19; 15:1–3.

33. See Thomas C. Oden, *Radical Obedience* (Philadelphia: Westminster Press, 1964), pp. 44f.

34. Rudolf Bultmann, "Grace and Freedom," *Essays*, pp. 168–81; "On Behalf of Christian Freedom," *Existence and Faith*, pp. 241–47.

35. Bultmann, *Existence and Faith*, pp. 241f.

36. Ibid. p. 144.

37. Bultmann, *Theology of the New Testament*, I, 331.

38. Ibid., p. 287.   39. Ibid., pp. 331f.

40. Bultmann, "New Testament and Mythology," p. 41.

41. Bultmann, *Theology of the New Testament*, I, 340; see also "Christ the End of the Law," pp. 36–66.

42. Bultmann, *Theology of the New Testament*, I, 342.

43. Bultmann, *Existence and Faith*, p. 255.

44. Ibid., p. 260.   45. Ibid.   46. Ibid.

47. Bultmann, *Theology of the New Testament*, I, 348.

48. Ibid.

49. Bultmann, *Existence and Faith*, p. 181.

50. Bultmann, "New Testament and Mythology," p. 2.

51. Bultmann, *Theology of the New Testament*, I, 329.

52. Ibid., II, 75ff.   53. Ibid., I, 278.   54. Ibid., p. 330.

55. Bultmann, *Jesus Christ and Mythology*, p. 81.

56. Bultmann, *Presence*, p. 41.   57. Ibid., pp. 43–46.

58. Bultmann, *Presence*, p. 48.

59. Bultmann, *Jesus Christ and Mythology*, p. 81.

60. Ibid., p. 82.   61. Ibid., p. 31.

62. Bultmann, "Bultmann Replies to His Critics," p. 205.

CHAPTER X

1 Bultmann, *Essays*, p. 88.   2. Ibid., pp. 79f.

3. Joseph Fletcher, *Situation Ethics* (Philadelphia: The Westminster Press, 1966), pp. 33f.; see John A. T. Robinson, *Honest To God* (London: SCM Press Ltd., 1963), pp. 116ff. for his "love only" norm in ethics.

4. I have discussed these at the end of chapter V above.

5. Schubert M. Ogden, *Christ Without Myth* (New York: Harper & Bros., 1961), pp. 112f.

6. Ibid., p. 124.

7. Günther Bornkamm, *Jesus of Nazareth*, trans. Irene and Fraser McLuskey with James M. Robinson (New York: Harper & Bros., 1960).

8. Kegley, op. cit., p. 177.

9. Bultmann, *Jesus Christ and Mythology*, p. 69.

10. S. Paul Schilling, *Contemporary Continental Theologians* (Nashville and New York: Abingdon Press, 1966), p. 100.

11. Bultmann, *Jesus and the Word*, pp. 84f.

12. Bultmann, *Essays*, p. 7.   13. Macquarrie, op. cit., p. 215.

14. Bultmann, *Existence and Faith*, p. 140.

15. Ibid., p. 201.   16. Schilling, op. cit., p. 96.

17. 2 Cor. 5:19; Phil. 2:5–11; John 1:14; 10:30; 14:9.

18. John Macquarrie, *The Scope of Demythologizing* (London: SCM Press Ltd., 1960), p. 21.

Selected Bibliography

The present bibliography is very brief. For more detailed bibliography see the footnotes, and the volumes cited in footnote no. 6 in chapter I.

VOLUMES BY BULTMANN

Essays: Philosophical and Theological. Translated by James C. G. Greig. London: SCM Press, 1955.

Das Evangelium des Johannes. Göttingen: Vandenhoeck & Ruprecht, 1941.

Existence and Faith. Translated by Schubert M. Ogden. Cleveland and New York: The World Publishing Company, 1960.

Faith and Understanding, I. Translated by Louise Pettibone Smith. New York and Evanston: Harper & Row, 1969. Essays from *Glauben und Verstehen,* I.

Glauben und Verstehen, I (1933), II (1952), III (1960), IV (1965) Tübingen: J. C. B. Mohr (Paul Siebeck).

The Gospel of John, A Commentary. Translated by G. R. Beasley-Murray. Philadelphia: The Westminster Press, 1971.

The History of the Synoptic Tradition. Translated by John Marsh. Oxford: Basil Blackwell, 1963.

Jesus and the Word. Translated by Louise Pettibone Smith and Erminie Huntress Lantero. New York: Charles Scribner's Sons, 1958.

Jesus Christ and Mythology. New York: Charles Scribner's Sons, 1958.

The Old and New Man. Translated by Keith R. Crim. Richmond: John Knox Press, 1967.

Primitive Christianity in Its Contemporary Setting. Translated by
R. H. Fuller. Cleveland and New York: The World Publishing
Company, 1956.
The Presence of Eternity, History and Eschatology. New York:
Harper & Bros., 1957.
Theology of the New Testament. 2 vols. Translated by Kendrick
Grobel. New York: Charles Scribner's Sons, 1951 and 1955.
This World and the Beyond. Translated by Harold Knight. New
York: Charles Scribner's Sons, 1960.

OTHER ESSAYS OF BULTMANN

Bultmann's essays are numerous. Three volumes are listed above:
Faith and Understanding (Vol. I of *Glauben und Verstehen*); *Existence and Faith* which includes some of *Glauben und Verstehen*, III;
and *Essays: Philosophical and Theological* which is *Glauben und
Verstehen*, II. The following essays are listed because of their importance and their availability to English readers.

"General Truths and Christian Proclamation." In *History and Hermeneutic*, edited by Robert W. Funk, translated by Schubert M.
Ogden, pp. 153–62. New York: Harper & Row, 1967.

"The Idea of God and Modern Man." In *Journal for Theology and
the Church*, vol. 2. *Translating Theology into the Modern Age*,
edited by Robert W. Funk, pp. 89–95. New York: Harper & Row,
1965. Reprint edition published by Peter Smith, Magnolia, Mass.
The essay also appears in R. Gregor Smith, ed., *The World Come
of Age* (Philadelphia: Fortress Press, 1967), pp. 256–74.

"New Testament and Mythology." In *Kerygma and Myth*, edited
by Hans Werner Bartsch; translated by Reginald H. Fuller, pp.
1–44. London: S.P.C.K., 1960. See also "Bultmann Replies to
his Critics," pp. 191–211 in the same volume.

"The Primitive Christian Kerygma and the Historical Jesus." In
The Historical Jesus and the Kerygmatic Christ, edited and trans-
lated by Carl E. Braaten and Roy A. Harrisville. New York and
Nashville: Abingdon Press, 1964.

"The Significance of the Old Testament for the Christian Faith."
In *The Old Testament and Christian Faith*, edited by B. W. Anderson. New York: Harper & Row; London: SCM Press, 1963.

"What Sense Is There to Speak of God?" *The Christian Scholar* 43
(1960), 213–22.

HELPFUL WORKS ON BULTMANN AND HIS THEOLOGY

HENDERSON, IAN. Rudolf Bultmann. London: Lutterworth Press, 1965.

KEGLEY, CHARLES W., ed. *The Theology of Rudolf Bultmann.* New York: Harper & Row, 1966.

MACQUARRIE, JOHN. *An Existentialist Theology.* New York and Evanston: Harper & Row, 1955.

————. *The Scope of Demythologizing.* London: SCM Press, 1960.

OGDEN, THOMAS C. *Radical Obedience.* Philadelphia: The Westminster Press, 1964.

OGDEN, SCHUBERT M. *Christ Without Myth.* New York: Harper & Bros., 1961.

PERRIN, NORMAN. *The Promise of Bultmann.* Philadelphia and New York: J. B. Lippincott Company, 1969.

ROBINSON, JAMES M. *The Bultmann School of Biblical Interpretation: New Directions?* New York: Harper & Row, 1965.

SCHILLING, S. PAUL. *Contemporary Continental Theologians.* Nashville and New York: Abingdon Press, 1966. The chapter on Bultmann is superb.

SCHMITHALS, WALTER. *An Introduction to the Theology of Rudolf Bultmann.* London: SCM Press, 1968. This is the best "Introduction" to Bultmann of which I know.